FIFTIES

Fords

an illustrated history of the 1950's Fords

By **RAY MILLER**

with Photographs by **GLENN EMBREE**

THE EVERGREEN PRESS
Avalon, California

THE NIFTY FIFTIES *Ford*

Library of Congress Catalog Card Number 73-93879
ISNB 0-913056-05-7

First Printing December 1974
Seventh Printing June 1987

Copyright Ray Miller 1974

Printed by:
Sierra Printers, Inc.
Bakersfield, California

printed in U.S.A.

The Evergreen Press
Avalon, California

RAY MILLER, along with Bruce McCalley, another Founding Member of the Model T Ford Club of America, produced *FROM HERE TO OBSCURITY*, a book that has become the Standard Reference for those interested in the Model T Ford. From that effort it was a relatively modest step to apply similar techniques of reporting to the pre-war Ford V-8 and the result was *THE V-8 AFFAIR* which became the "bible" for those interested in the early "flathead" engine. *HENRY'S LADY*, a similar work detailing the Model A Ford continued the precedent set earlier, and the three books have been described as "the greatest collection of detailed information on the 1906-1942 Ford automobiles". Later, in 1973, the three were joined in *The Ford Road Series* by a similarly comprehensive work entitled *THUNDERBIRD!* which covered the Ford-T-birds as they have never before been done.

Ray has, in his younger days, owned many early Fords, and has continued his interest in the Ford through recent years. His collection at this time includes a 1910 Model T Ford, a restored 1936 Phaeton, a 1954 Skyliner, and not one, but *two*, 1957 Thunderbirds!

In addition to having had the responsibility for the text and the production of this book, it was Ray who located the cars used to illustrate this work. His ability to find exactly the right cars is enhanced by the fact that in Southern California there are so many original, unrestored and un-modified cars still being driven daily on the freeways. The climate in Southern California thus has a great deal to do with the availability of subject material.

GLENN EMBREE, well known to readers of *THE VINTAGE FORD*, served as President of the Model T Ford Club of America, and has, since its inception provided the reknown colorful covers for that outstanding magazine. Fundamentally a Photographic Essayist, Glenn has been involved with photography both as a hobby, and as a Profession, since 1940.

Co-Author, with Ray Miller, of *THE V-8 AFFAIR, HENRY'S LADY*, and *THUNDERBIRD!* Glenn has established an enviable pattern of photographic reporting which is continued in this book. Although his Studio in Hollywood, California, is adorned with portraits of well-known celebrities, it is apparent that Glenn *enjoys* his automotive portraiture as the results exhibit an interest and excitment that would otherwise be lacking.

Glenn has had a long-continuing relationship with the Ford Motor Company, in particular during the period here under study. His work was frequently employed by the Company in their advertising material and readers of this book will note the use in several instances of some of the promotional-type photographs of the 1954-59 cars that were *originally* shot by Glenn in contemporary times.

The Authors wish to thank the many people whose acceptance of the concept of such a book was expressed by their willingness and enthusiasm in assisting the project. The Owners are generally mentioned by name within the text, but again we wish to thank them for their interest, their cooperation, and their patience while we scrambled around, over, through, and under their cars obtaining the pictures we used here. Additionally, we want to thank:

THE FORD MOTOR COMPANY for their cooperation in preparing this book, and their enthusiastic promotion of the earlier books in The Ford Road series. Literature provided by the Company has greatly aided the pursuit of accuracy in connection with the text.

The Parts Department staff at DIXON FORD in Carlsbad, California was extremely anxious to assist us by confirming part numbers, usage, application, and even availability of many parts. Their help went far in establishing authenticity of many questionable examples.

BILL NORTON of *Valley Obsolete Ford Parts*, North Hollywood, California, HAROLD LOONEY of *Vintage Auto Parts*, Orange, California, and GENE VALDEZ of *Ford Parts Obsolete* of Long Beach, California, all opened their showrooms to our cameras, and CHARLIE JONES of *Obsolete Ford Parts* of Nashville, Georgia, and DEAN MCDONALD of Rockport, Indiana both were able to supply scarce parts for our 1954 "bubbletop" from their seemingly inexhaustible stock.

JIM PETRIK of Madeira, Ohio, whose personal devotion to Ford may only be exceeded by that of the Author, provided many obscure but relevent facts as well as a large supply of his personal reference material. His correspondence frequently provoked an extensive additional research to validate a point.

LARRY BLODGETT, founder, and first President of the *Fabulous Fifties Ford Club of America*, an enthusiastic and devoted Fifties Ford-watcher approved of the project and greatly assisted by referring the author to exemplary cars for illustrative purposes. In addition, Larry opened his noted collection of Miniatures to our cameras for the interesting study which is included in this book. Members of the Fabulous Fifties Ford Club of America on several occasions convened expressly for our convenience and we again note our gratitude to them.

And to . . . Professor David L. Lewis of Ann Arbor, Michigan whose intellectual curiosity was penetrating enough and whose persistance was firm enough to result in the production figures expressed *by model* which appear later in this book.

In preparing this material, the authors have attempted to locate unrestored, low mileage original cars wherever possible. Failing in this, we have employed as models, restorations believed to be of the highest quality. Our gratitude is extended to the owners of all of these cars.

As is to be expected, there may well be items of incorrect date or style on a given automobile. Original automobiles may well have been modified to suit the convenience of earlier owners; restorations are generally done to the best level of information available to the restorer, but occasionally a slip-up, sometimes of frightening proportions will occur.

We have attempted to screen the inaccuracies; we hope that we may have succeeded in that effort. This book was intended to be what it is, a copendium of information which will enable an observer to identify, and to classify both cars and parts. If there are errors, they are not to our knowlege.

The Authors

Lula Belle, a 6-cylinder '53 Mainline Tudor, wasn't my first car, or even my first postwar Ford (I'd previously owned a '51 Customline Victoria). But she was the only car my wife and I have ever given a name. She was our honeymoon car, and eventually we filled her with four kids, and toured most of the country. That overdrive finally paid off!

When I went to work for GM in 1959, plain, high-riding Lula Belle went with me—right into the GM Tech Center and other sancrosanct places where Fords had never gone before. My associates were tolerantly amused, knowing that I'd been a penniless graduate student, and couldn't afford a new GM car right off. Eventually I bought GM. But Lula Belle was kept for sentimental reasons until 1964, when my wife, casting sentiment aside, questioned the wisdom of driving a car whose defroster wouldn't work, doors wouldn't close, etc. So we sold Lula Belle to a college kid for 50 bucks; and when he drove away the lump in my throat was so big I had to unbutton my collar. To this day when I see a blue '53 Mainline, pleasant memories wash over me. It's as if I've seen a high school sweetheart, and she's even prettier than I remembered her. Come through these pages with me, share my fond memories of Lula Belle and other Nifty Fifties Fords, and you'll know what I mean.

David L. Lewis
Professor of Business History
The University of Michigan

"It Happened in Sun Valley", the title of a long-forgotten song could well be the title of this photograph, because it *was* shot in Sun Valley, Idaho, in the summer of 1954 by Glenn Embree.

Posed for possible use in forth-coming Company advertising material, the effect of the sharp, new, Sunliner in its exciting new Goldenrod Yellow and Raven Black colors and matching interior was further heightened by the optional accessory wire wheel covers.

Glenn's special ability to pose a number of people with an automobile and to tie the result together to look like an unplanned snapshot was never more apparent than in this twenty-year-old photograph, for even the spectacle of a swan-like female ice-skater at the near-center of the photograph does little to distract attention from the beautiful new Ford.

On June 21, 1945, "The Smiling Irishman", a used car dealer in New York City, was accused by the Assistant United States Attorney of having sold a 1940 sedan to a returning war veteran at some $270 above the OPA Ceiling price. According to the complaint, the total price was $599.

Twenty-Nine years later, according to a consensus taken from the advertising columns of several popular antique automobile publications, the same car would bring up to $2500. Apparently, The Smiling Irishman didn't sell too **high**, just too soon!

This book is therefore dedicated to Mr. Robert Kuranoff who in 1945 conducted his used car business at the corner of Eighth Avenue and 53rd Street in New York City under the trade name of "The Smiling Irishman".

The Authors wish to give thanks to the Owners of cars featured in this work. No attempt has been made to isolate the cars. Since we have been attempting to describe the *characteristics* of a given year, we have deliberately employed those pictures which best served the immediate purpose. *For this reason, adjacent photos may not necessarily show views of the same car.*

CONTENTS

"The colorful new coat of arms was derived by the styling department from a crest dating back to 17th century England. It appears on the front of the hood directly over the center of the grille, and on the center of the trunk lid over the handle.

The crest is in the shape of a shield, surmounted by the word "Ford" in block letters on a black background. It is divided into three fields of red, white, and blue, separated by a black chevron marked with five gold spheres. Three golden lions are mounted, one in the center of each of the fields.

The late Henry Ford had never developed a crest for his car, but had nevertheless been interested in the heraldry of the Ford family since early in the century. Research into that and other aspects of the family history revealed that the Fords had lived for many generations in Ireland, having originally moved there from the vicinity of Somersetshire and Devonshire in England. Mr. Ford's father, William, came to America in 1847 from County Cork, Ireland, and settled on a farm in Wayne County, Michigan. This research contributed to the development of the new crest."

FROM *FORD TIMES*, October 1949

At 10:50 AM, on July 3, 1945, only weeks after an expiring War Production Board (WPB) had given final authority to the Industry to manufacture civilian automobiles, Henry Ford II, then Vice President of the Ford Motor Company, drove the first post-war Ford, (and the first of **any** *manufacturer), a Super Deluxe Tudor sedan off the assembly line line at the Rouge. Assembled newsmen reportedly saw a total of 23* **more** *cars on the lines that morning.*

This first car was presented later that summer to President Harry S. Truman by Mr. Ford on behalf of his grandfather. The first **purchased** *post-war Ford went, on October 24, 1945, to Lt. John C. Sjogren, Congressional Medal of Honor winner, of Rockford, Michigan for whom it was purchased by donations from most of Rockford's 2500 residents.*

HISTORY

Incorporated in Delaware, July 9, 1919, and subsequently acquired all the assets of Ford Motor Company, organized in Michigan, June 16, 1903. The predecessor company was capitalized for $100,000 of which only $28,000 in cash was actually paid in. There were 12 stockholders, including Henry Ford who held a 25% interest. In 1908, Henry Ford increased his holdings to 51% and shortly thereafter to 58½%. In 1919, Edsel B. Ford, who had succeeded his father as president, purchased the outstanding minority interest of 41½%.

On February 4, 1922, acquired at receiver's sale assets of the Lincoln Motor Co. which was incorporated in 1917. On April 1, 1922, organized the Lincoln Motor Co. under Michigan laws, which company was dissolved in 1940. The Lincoln plant is now operated as a department of Ford Motor Co.

BUSINESS & PRODUCTS

Normal Operations: Company is primarily engaged in the manufacture and sale of automobiles, producing the "Ford," "Mercury," "Lincoln," "Lincoln Continental" and "Lincoln Custom" lines of passenger cars, the "Ford" line of commercial cars and the "Ford" bus chassis. The predecessor company sold its first automobile in July, 1903, and there had been built and sold more than 30,000,000 Ford cars and trucks by Feb., 1942.

Company has also been engaged at times in the past in the manufacture of tractors and airplanes. In the spring of 1939 it started production at the Rouge plant in Dearborn of a new line of lightweight tractors and implements, under license from Harry Ferguson, Ltd., distribution being handled by Harry Ferguson, Inc.

Company produces a considerable portion of the raw materials and parts used in the production of its motor cars. It manufactures and either uses or sells numerous by-products. Affiliated activities include the operation of coke ovens, blast furnaces, steel mills, glass factories, paper mills, cement plants, etc. Miscellaneous activities include the operation of machine shops, electric power plants, ocean vessels, lake freighters and barges.

There are various associated companies in foreign countries which have contract rights to make "Ford" products and market such products in designated territory. Such concerns have manufacturing plants at Windsor, Canada; Dagenham, England; Asnieres, France; and Cologne, Germany.

1946 Moody's Industrial Manual, Page 2379

On February 10, 1942, a 1942 Super DeLuxe Fordor sedan was rolled off of the end of the assembly line at the Ford plant in Dearborn signifying the conversion of the plant's effort to a military support mission. For the next four years, Ford was to devote its activities exclusively to the manufacture of trucks, planes, personnel carriers, Jeeps (originally designed by Willys, but second-sourced by Ford), and other military vehicles.

During this time the civilian population was greatly reduced by the call to arms of over 5,000,000 men and women who were brought into uniform in a totally dedicated effort to defeat the Axis forces. Actually two separate wars were being fought, one with Italy and Germany in Europe and Africa, and the other with Japan in the Pacific. Although under one leadership, and with one devotion, the Army, in characteristic euphemism referred to the "European Theater" and the Pacific Theater" wars which for the next few years were to occupy the total concentration of the country.

As will be imagined, shortages developed. Meat, sugar, butter and other dairy products came into short supply and were rationed as were automobile tires, the remaining stocks of civilian automobiles, and finally gasoline. The well-remembered "A" Gasoline sticker entitled each citizen to a total ration of *two gallons* per week, and commercial users were given "C" stamps worth only 5 gallons each.

Even with this cut-back in automobile usage, it is obvious that time alone takes its toll and by 1945, with no civilian passenger cars having been produced for the preceeding three years, even the people at home, collectively speaking, were in need, or so they believed, of "new cars". For over ten years previous to the cut-off, it was the policy of the manufacturers to generate their new market by modifying the *appearance* of their cars, and although this in itself would not have caused "need" for a new car, promotional advertising and publicity made the next year's car appear to be so vastly superior to the previous model that many were coherced into believing that after only a year or two an automobile was worth little but the down payment on a new one. Thus even if some 5,000,000 soldier-citizens were not to return to the market shortly, even without them there was a substantial demand for new cars.

On April 13, 1945, Franklin Delano Roosevelt, who had served his country as President for 12 years and who was only about 100 days into his unprecedented fourth term, died and Harry S. Truman was sworn in as the nation's 33rd President. Events were moving fast then, almost too fast to follow, and, in the next few weeks, Nuremberg fell, then Bologna, Stuttgart, and Russian troops entering Berlin itself. Germany crumbled rapidly, and on April 30th, Italian patriots took their revenge on Italian dictator Benito Mussolini; the U.S. 5th army entered Milan, the 7th Army captured Munich. On May 2nd, German forces in Italy and Austria surrendered to the Allies, and on the 8th, Germany surrendered unconditionally.

On May 9th, Harry S. Truman proclaimed V-8 Day, and the end to the conflicts that beset us was in sight. True, the Pacific Theater war continued to rage, but with the availability of the Army that had just defeated the mightiest war machine ever known to man, it was a foregone conclusion that a victory in the Pacific was at hand.

In this period, agencies of the Federal Governemnt such as the War Production Board (WPB), and the Office of Price Administration (OPA) had been charged with the responsibility for allocating strategic materials and ascertaining that they were sold at a "fair" price. In general a creditable job was done as viewed by the results, although there are those who would argue that these agencies were continued beyond their useful life. In any event, acting on the authority delegated to them, on June 21st, 1945, the WPB announced an *increase* in civilian auto output for the second half of the year. This was the first public confirmation of what was thus obvious: an *increase* for the second half of the year could only follow a beginning in the first half, and although there was not yet available information on exactly what Detroit was doing, it became clear to those who were watching that Detroit had already embarked on the retooling for civilian production!

And then, on July 3, 1945, The Ford Motor Company once again scooped the industry by producing the first post-war automobile to be assembled! Driven off the end of an assembly line (it was reported that there were over 20 additional cars visible at that moment) by Henry Ford II, newly released from the United States Navy to assist his aging grandfather in the operation of the Ford automotive empire, the car created the sort of splash and interest that Ford must have anticipated.

While not at all a "new model" in any real sense, the car was typical of the style that was to be produced for the next three years until production was able to catch up with demand. With demand evident for hundreds of thousand Ford cars, there was little justification for holding off production just then to await a "new" design. Rather, it was truly a matter of competitive survival that dictated the need for Ford to merely face-lift their 1942 model, dust off the tooling and rush back into production.

So it was that on July 4th, 1945, newspapers all over the country tantalized their readers with a photograph of Henry Ford II driving what was variously described as a "1945" and a "1946" model Tudor sedan. In all, some 35,000 cars of similar appearance would be built in the balance of the calendar year, and every single one of them would find a willing and anxious owner.

Shortages of new vehicles was to some extent caused by the fact that some items continued to be "controlled" by the WPB or the OPA, and others did not. Prices of these new vehicles were related by the OPA to the 1942 models although with an expanding, and inflationary, economy, it was clear that labor would not accept 1942 wages as adequate. Hence the production of these new cars faltered and although gas rationing ended on August 16th and on August 25th the WPB revoked all controls on passenger car output (this did not alter the OPA pricing position, merely allowed the Company to *build* all the cars it wanted to or *could*), on September 22nd, the Company announced that the Public showing of the new 1946 passenger cars was to be indefinitely postponed due to growing number of strikes. Rumors circulated widely, but were denied by the OPA, that prices for the new cars would be as much as 25% higher than those of the '42. No one seemed yet to know where to go or when to go, and by now V-J Day had been declared (9/2), and returning veterans were swelling the demand for automobiles.

PUBLICITY RELEASE
(#175)

September 20, 1945

NATIONAL SHOWING POSTPONED

National public showing of the 1946 Ford automobiles has been postponed indefinitely, J. R. Davis, director of sales and advertising of the Ford Motor Company, today notified dealers throughout the nation.

Mr. Davis said that although the nation is sorely in need of new automobiles, the Ford company will have to continue to keep its production operations closed because of strikes that have shut down many of the company's major suppliers.

Mr. Davis said the public showing originally had been set for September 21.

Ford's first post-war offering was this "slab-sided" 1949 Fordor sedan. The first Ford to eliminate the discernible fenders, it was the start of the "fifties" styling and marked an abrupt departure from past designs. A milepost in its own right, the 1949 Ford was truly the start of the "modern" designs and all successive models through the 1950's were derived from this car rather than the earlier pre-war styling which was more closely linked to the past.

Chaos, of course, was to follow. Cars would be built, but not under the controls. Labor could receive a satisfactory wage, but not under controls. Manufacturers could sell their products, but not under controls. Strikes were everywhere; (on September 21st, Ford reported that due to strikes only 2,312 passenger cars had been built since July 3rd in place of 10,000 scheduled) limiting the components, as well as the finished product, and through it all, bureacratic experts persisted in their task of holding the price line. Conflicts of ideology caused shortened tempers and for the next several months almost no "ordinary" guy received a new car despite the agonizing low, but respectable 35,000 units produced.

These early post-war problems were solved! Some say that time itself provided the solution. Late in 1948, Ford previewed a straight-sided car, minimizing fenders as such, and with the beginnings of a new post-war "modern" look about it. Year by year the design was refined and the basic car enlarged. Engines were made more powerful, and optional power accessories were provided to control these new behemoths of the road. An ever-enlarging spiral had begun, culminating in the 118" wheel base Galaxie of 1959, sculptured giants far removed from the *early* post war Fords.

Let us proceed then with the study of these changes and a recording of the growth. Let us now pursue . . .

"The Nifty Fifties Fords"

One of the best looking of all of the Ford-produced Convertibles, this 1955 model sports the new Fairlane trim including the chromed "brow" over the headlights and the rakish "check mark" stripe down the sides. Note the standard hub caps used in this photograph and the original wide white sidewall tires.

"THERE'S A FORD IN YOUR FUTURE"

From the initial assembly of a post-war Ford on July 3, 1945, to the end of that year approximately 35,000 cars were completed. However, almost no one bothers to designate them as "1945" models for in the chaos immediately following the war most of them were produced in the last quarter of the year and obviously became known as "1946" models. Thus the post-war Fords emerged as the "1946" Ford, and since all were manufactured to the same design anyway, those early post-war cars lost their initial designation and have become known only as "the 1946 model".

*Commercially, it really made no difference because customers were lining up at the Dealer's to place their orders, and all that they wanted was a new Ford, **not** a "1945" or a "1946" model.*

*The post-war Ford was fundamentally a 1942 model; the pressures of the times demanding the prompt manufacture of **cars**, and Ford did the obvious, they manufactured the earlier car with only a few trim items changed to mark it as somehow "different". Two lines were offered, and initially a total of ten passenger car body styles including a sedan delivery to which an eleventh, the wooden-bodied Sportsman Convertible was added late in 1946. However, under the circumstances, it was not easy for customers to make model selections.*

By the end of 1945, some 680,000 back orders existed and only about 35,000 cars had been shipped. Even at the end of 1946, Ford had shipped only about 400,000 of the model, so it becomes clear that their well-intentioned advertising slogan, "There's a Ford in your future" did, in irritatingly concise terms, describe about one out of three who had placed their orders for the new Ford.

100 H.P. V-8 ENGINE: The most powerful engine ever to power a Ford car. Incorporates improved manifolds, new valve cooling and higher capacity oil pump, plus other improvements affecting virtually every operating part of the engine. Combines unusual performance with unusual economy.

90 H.P. SIX ENGINE: The most modern Six in the low-price field. Further refined by new valve cooling, new manifolding and a host of other improvements for record performance with outstanding economy.

IMPROVED COOLING: Both Six and V-8 engines feature improved valve seat cooling; new pressure-valve radiator cap permits higher operating temperature for increased efficiency; minimizes loss of water and anti-freeze due to evaporation. New center-point mounting stabilizes radiator, protecting it from road shocks.

SMOOTHER RIDE: Long, slow-action springs of new multi-leaf design smoother smallest road irregularities, result in a smoother, more level ride. Fabric-lined metal covers (on Super De Luxe) retain lubricant for uniform spring action, keep road dirt and water out. These, combined with 125-inch spring base, adjustable, double-acting hydraulic shock absorbers and low center of gravity, set a new standard in riding comfort.

NEW STABILITY: Two-way stabilization imparts new roadability and handling ease when rounding curves or driving in a crosswind. Transverse stabilizers, front and rear, preserve alignment between axles and frame, reduce sidesway. Torsional stabilizer on front controls spring action, prevents "roll," keeps car on even keel when driving on rough roads, improving stability and riding comfort.

NEW SELF-CENTERING HYDRAULIC BRAKES: Oversized brakes with 162 square inches of lining area, larger than in some higher priced cars, provide powerful straightline stopping action with long lining life. New self-centering feature insures positive shoe alignment for smooth, *quiet action* with soft pedal pressure.

NEW ELECTRICAL SYSTEM: Engines are equipped with new heat and ozone resistant wiring, waterproof ignition coil and distributor. Full automatic and vacuum control permits best over-all performance and economy on standard grades of fuel with freedom from "ping" or detonation. New *long-life* voltage regulator automatically controls generator output to maintain battery in a charged condition.

TORQUE-TUBE DRIVE: with front radius rods—the backbone of the Ford stabilized chassis. All driving and braking forces are transmitted directly to the frame. Springs are unrestricted in their action to support load and cushion road shocks for smooth, easy, riding comfort.

BODY TYPES: *Super De Luxe Body Types:* Tudor Sedan, Fordor Sedan, Coupe, Sedan-Coupe, Convertible Club Coupe, Station Wagon. *De Luxe Body Types:* Tudor Sedan, Fordor Sedan, Coupe.

NEW BRIGHT COLORS: Both De Luxe and Super De Luxe Ford cars are available in a range of optional colors at no extra cost. All colors are enduring, hi-gloss baked enamel, highly resistant to fogging or dimming.

UPHOLSTERY: *Super De Luxe:* Choice of Broadcloth or Mohair in combination gray and gray striped pattern. Golden tan, red or blue genuine leather seats in Convertible Club Coupe. Golden tan genuine leather seats in Station Wagon. *De Luxe Models:* Choice of tan striped Mohair or Broadcloth.

WHEELS and TIRES: Five, pressed steel, curved disc type, with 4-inch width rims. 6.00 x 16, 4-ply tires on passenger cars—6-ply on Station Wagons.

DE LUXE EQUIPMENT: (Items marked with asterisk * are in Super De Luxe only.) Front and rear bumpers and four bumper guards. Spare wheel. Twin air-electric horns. Two combination tail lamps and stop lamps. Dual windshield wipers with speed control on instrument panel. *Electric cigar lighter. *Two sun visors. Foot control for sealed-beam headlamps with

indicator on instrument panel. Dimming control for instrument panel lights. Ignition keyhole light. Glove compartment with lock. *Two ash trays on instrument panel. Leather-covered arm rests in sedan rear seats. Arm rest on driver's side of front seat. Inside hood lock. Separate parking lamps. Plastic radio speaker grille when radio equipped. Foot rests in Fordor sedans. Friction type door checks. Automatic light in luggage compartment. Rubber mat on luggage compartment floor. *Instrument panel clock. *Horn ring on steering wheel. *Crank control for front door ventilators. *Ash tray in rear of sedans. *Assist cords. *Robe cord in Fordor sedans. *Leather-covered arm rests on both front doors. Bright finish interior hardware

TRADITIONAL FORD QUALITY: Backed by over 40 years' manufacturing experience, the Ford in Your Future combines all the craftsmanship and knowledge of metallurgy acquired in the building of over 31,000,000 vehicles. Quality of materials was never higher; manufacturing precision is of the traditional Ford standard—the highest in the industry. These new Ford cars are finer in quality, performance and stamina than any previous model.

ACCESSORIES: Wide range. Engineered and especially built for Ford cars. Available at moderate cost. Ford Adjust-O-Matic Radio with foot control and Touch-Bar tuning. Improved Hot-Water and Hot-Air Heaters and Defrosters.

A new advertising slogan, "There's a Ford in Your Future" was illustrated by a hand holding a crystal ball in which the new Ford was to be seen. With the long waiting period that developed between the placing of an order and the delivery of a car, the slogan became abrasively prophetic and exasperating to those who were on the long "waiting lists". A Ford Motor Company advertisement early in November, 1945, reported a total of 326,840 back orders, and later, according to the Detroit News on December 8th, the list had grown to over 680,000 orders!

FORD PASSENGER CAR MODELS

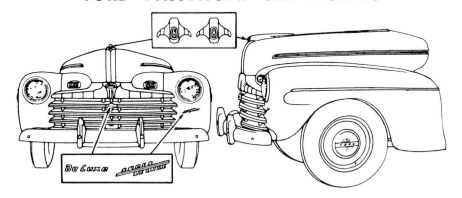

MODEL 69A FORD DELUXE OR SUPER DELUXE—100 HP. 8-Cylinder Engine
MODEL 6GA FORD DELUXE OR SUPER DELUXE—90 HP. 6-Cylinder Engine
(114″ Wheelbase)

BODY TYPE	NAME	BODY TYPE	NAME
70-A	De Luxe Tudor Sedan	76	Super De Luxe Convertible Club Coupe
70-B	Super De Luxe Tudor Sedan	77-A	De Luxe (5-Window) Coupe
71	Sportsman Coupe	77-B	Super De Luxe (5-Window) Coupe
72-B	Super De Luxe Sedan Coupe		
73-A	De Luxe Fordor Sedan	78	De Luxe Sedan Delivery
73-B	Super De Luxe Fordor Sedan	79-B	Super De Luxe Station Wagon

1946 Type 76 Convertible Club Coupe

1946 Type 73 Fordor Sedan

A great similarity existed between the 1942 and the post-war 1946 models. Dimensionally they were about the same, although with the new grill treatment in which horizontal lines were emphasized, the later cars did appear wider.

Parking light placement and general overall design features of the 1946 car follow those of the earlier 1942 models (right).

The grill of the 1942 model, shown for comparison, is composed of a number of vertical bars; other features resemble the 1946 cars.

The 1946 hood ornament (right) bears the applicable 6 or 8 depending on engine selection. It is flared and more elaborate than the 1942 style (above).

The Ford name is emplaced on the upper grill bar in 1946, and the hood has no further emblem. In 1942 (right) a separate emblem bearing the name was placed just below the hood ornament.

Although both parking lights are rectangular, and both are installed in the fenders *between* the headlights, the 1946 style (right) differs from the earlier ones (above).

1946 TYPE 76 SUPER DE LUXE CONVERTIBLE CLUB COUPE *Mr. Jack Story, Fallbrook, California*

Perhaps the most eagerly sought of all of the early post-war models was the sporty Convertible Club Coupe. While hardly a new design, it continued to appeal to both the younger element and the Country Club set. Comfortably seating five, and capable of six, the Convertible Club Coupe remains to this day a highly prized automobile.

The Motor-Lift Top is operated by hydraulic cylinders controlled by a knob mounted under the dashboard. The snug fitting canvas top is manually latched at the front header.

Rear quarter windows rotate to open, and the "window post" is formed by self-mounted stainless channels on both windows.

A graceful outside door handle is matched to the lines of the body side trim.

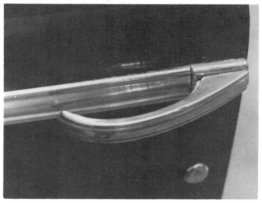

Vent windows in the Super De Luxe line are crank-operated. De Luxe series cars are manually opened.

Dual windshield wipers are standard on both series, as is the bright metal trim around the windshield.

The cowl ventilator is continued unchanged. Operated by a handle suspended beneath the dashboard, it provides a cooling flow of air through a wire bug screen.

The winged, chrome-plated, hood ornament shows either a 6 or an 8 indicating the engine choice in the particular car.

A rubber gravel guard, first added on the 1942 model is continued with no change on the 1946 rear fenders.

The grooved headlamp "door" is common to 1942 and 1946 (some late 1942 models were furnished with painted rather than plated doors) and is conspicuous by the annular grooves.

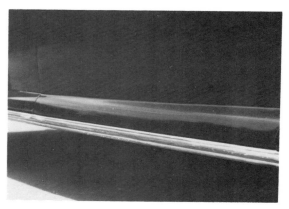

A lower chrome trim extends the length of the body but does not extend to the fenders.

As on the 1942 Model, beaded (grooved) fender moulding is used on the fenders as decorative trim, (there is no joint beneath it). A matching strip is affixed to the rear fenders.

Ford script appears on the upper grill trim.

The distinctive 1946 front end

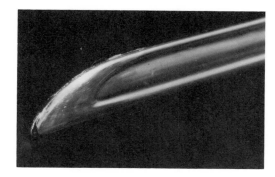

The grooved trim pieces on the hood have a characteristic pattern exclusive to 1946.

This parking light assembly is used in 1946 only.

Four bumper guards are included as standard bumper parts and are not accessories.

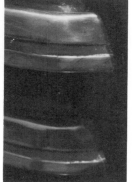

The horizontal grill trim pieces are grooved and the indented portion painted red.

If appropriate, the Super DeLuxe logo is emplaced beneath the left headlamp. DeLuxe series car are identified by the word displayed on the uppermost horizontal grill trim bar at the center, just below the Ford script emblem.

Wheels are pressed steel, 4" width rims, tires are 6:00 x 16, 4 ply (except Station Wagon which is 6 ply). The wide white side wall tires are optional accessories (black standard) as are the beauty rings.

The optional accessory wheel beauty rings have four concentric grooves.

Two combination tail-and stop-lamps are installed at the rear on all models as standard equipment. The rear lamps are identical with those used on the 1942 model (right).

The luggage compartment is furnished with an automatic light and a rubber mat. The locking handle is rotated to release the lid.

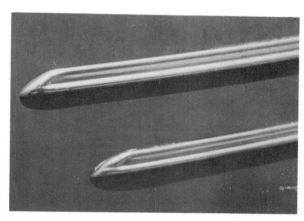

The luggage compartment lid is decorated with two trim strips formed with an embossed groove matching the trim strips on the front end. (page 33)

Standard equipment includes two front and two rear bumper guards, and the rear guards match the design of those in front.

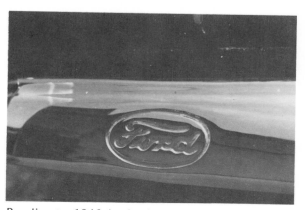

Peculiar to 1946 is the incorporation of the Ford script in the center of the rear bumper.

A lighted ignition lock is combined with a steering wheel lock which blocks the steering column when the key is withdrawn.

The steering wheel is disc-shaped and comparatively flat.

Horn rings are supplied only with the Super-DeLuxe series. Two interiors are offered in 1946, a blue-black color scheme in which the wheel is black, and a brown scheme (generally found on the DeLuxe series) in which a tan wheel is furnished.

Below the conventional LIGHT and THROTTLE knobs is the control knob for lowering the Convertible Club Coupe top.

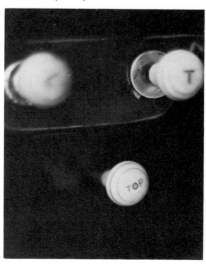

Matching ashtrays flank the radio speaker grill in the Super DeLuxe series. A sliding cover conceals the receptacle. The De Luxe series has one ash tray only, on the driver's side of the grill.

The radio is an optional accessory. In 1946, Ford's Adjust-O-Matic Radio featured touch-bar control and a foot-operated station selector.

Instrument faces are black, and on the Super De Luxe series the numerals and gradiants are highlighted in red. To the right of the electric clock (standard on the Super De Luxe; optional for the De Luxe) is a locking glove compartment. Below the clock is suspended the control switch for an accessory Hot-Water heater.

The shift lever knob is made of tan plastic.

The horn button, at the center of the wheel, bears a distinctive design. A horn ring is supplied on the Super De Luxe models only, but is an accessory for the De Luxe cars.

A non-Ford, but popular accessory for the model, is the chrome-plated metal dress-up trim set which replaces the stock plastic center grill and wings.

The hood, released from inside the car by means of a knob suspended under the dashboard, is hinged at the rear, opens from the front.

The Super De Luxe instruments are black-faced and highlighted in red. De Luxe instruments are also black-faced but do not have the red trim.

The electric clock is standard in the Super De Luxe series, but an optional accessory in the De Luxe series.

Four rectangular gauges appear to the left of the Speedometer in both series. These are the Fuel level, Oil pressure, Charge indicator, and radiator coolant Temperature.

The Temperature Gauge is adjusted to read "H" when the ignition key is turned off. Correct readings are obtained only with the instrument electrical circuit energized.

A pushbutton remote Starter switch is mounted at the left side, near the bottom, of the dashboard. Below it appears the hood latch release handle which is either grey or tan to correspond with the interior trim selection.

The Super De Luxe Fordor (and Tudor) sedan window area is outlined in a smooth chromed trim strip which is omitted on De Luxe models. The rear quarter windows of both the Fordor sedans pivot open for ventilation.

Matching door handles harmonize with the body side trim strips. A Keylock is furnished on each front door, but rear doors are locked only from the inside.

A distinct flare, or bulge, appears on the edge of the front fenders, just below the side trim strips.

Windshields are trimmed with bright metal strips on the Super De Luxe series, but this trim is omitted on De Luxe models.

1946 Type 70 Tudor Sedan

Mr. Bill Siebler, Torrance, California

A single, forward-facing, handle opens the wide doors. Beneath the handle is the keylock of which there are two, one on each door.

The ventilator in the front doors of the Super De Luxe cars is crank controlled (small handle below); De Luxe series was manually operated.

The inside handles furnished with the 1946 cars are: Door handle (top), Window riser (center) and ventilator (bottom). Chrome plated, the handles are fitted with plastic knobs and escutcheon plates.

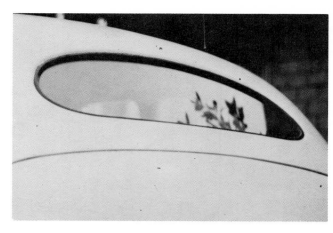

A wide, one-piece rear window is provided in sedans. There is no bright metal trim around the glass.

Fenders are secured to the body section with welting placed in the seam. The side trim continues almost to the luggage compartment lid.

The fuel filler pipe is reached through this access flap in the rear left fender.

1946 Type 79 B Super De Luxe Station Wagon

sun visor is an accessory

1946 Type 79 B Super De Luxe Station Wagon

Mr. Jeff Spellens, Reseda, California

Ford had pioneered in the factory-produced, wooden-bodied station wagons with the 1929 Model A version. Popularity of the versatile vehicle continued high through the pre-war years and the design was continued in 1946. Built to seat eight passengers and with removable second and third seats it could double as a cargo carrier of some capacity. It was, however, not normally employed in this manner but rather favored by the sporting set and it thus developed a sort of charisma which suggested a sort of luxury.

As with other cars in the Super De Luxe series, the ventilators in the front doors are cranked open. A manually operated safety lock is also provided.

Bodies of the Super De Luxe Station Wagon are made of maple with either birch or gum paneling. Below the wooden body is a trim strip (photo above) the design of which matches the fender trim strips.

Doors are hinged at the front to allow entry to both front and rear compartments at the same time.

All seats in the Super De Luxe Station Wagons are tan genuine leather and are installed without pleats or buttons.

An outside door handle, unique to the station wagon resembles that on the sedans (page 41) but is not interchangeable. Front doors are provided with keylocks.

Inside door panels are not upholstered. A door "pull" is provided on the rear doors as well as a door-locking lever.

Window glass in the rear doors, as well as that in the front, is lowered by a crank mechanism.

Sliding glass panel in the rear quarter is latched by a spring-loaded knob on the door post.

Two sun visors are provided. Note the construction of the roof which is formed of top material stretched over wooden battens and cross members.

Gussets are used to strengthen the rear corners. The rear window lifts outward and is supported, or latched, by tightening the knurled knob against the chromed slide track.

A dome light is placed above the second seat. The On/Off switch is part of the lamp.

A unique station wagon tail light bracket incorporates a pantograph arrangement to hold the light in the correct position regardless of the position of the tail gate.

The third seat is designed for three passengers; the second seat, narrower to allow entry to the rear, is for two only. The rear window is of two-piece construction.

FORD PASSENGER CAR MODELS

MODEL 79A FORD DELUXE OR SUPER DELUXE—100 HP. 8-Cylinder Engine

1947 **MODEL 7GA FORD DELUXE OR SUPER DELUXE—90 HP. 6-Cylinder Engine**

MODEL 7HA FORD DELUXE OR SUPER DELUXE—95 HP. 6-Cylinder Engine

1948 **MODEL 89A FORD DELUXE OR SUPER DELUXE—100 HP. 8-Cylinder Engine**

MODEL 8HA FORD DELUXE OF SUPER DELUXE—95 HP. 6-Cylinder Engine

(114″ Wheelbase)

BODY TYPE	NAME	BODY TYPE	NAME
70-A	De Luxe Tudor Sedan	76	Super De Luxe Convertible Club Coupe
70-B	Super De Luxe Tudor Sedan	77-A	De Luxe (5-Window) Coupe
71	Sportsman Coupe	77-B	Super De Luxe (5-Window) Coupe
72-B	Super De Luxe Sedan Coupe	78	De Luxe Sedan Delivery
73-A	De Luxe Fordor Sedan	79-B	Super De Luxe Station Wagon
73-B	Super De Luxe Fordor Sedan		

The 1947 Models were introduced in the Fall of 1946 at a time when Ford still had a substantial backlog (over 200,000 firm orders had yet to be filled) and Ford reacted by modifying still further the basic 1942 model that it had been producing. Little in the way of innovation was offered though and the eleven models of 1946 continued to be available with only changes in trim and parking light location to indicate a difference from the 1946 models.

If 1947 exhibited minimal change in style, 1948 was remarkable as offering even less. Aside from the elimination of the locking steering wheel ignition lock (and the relocation of the ignition switch to the dashboard) and a minor change in the cover of the outside door locks, as well as a relocation of the horn mountings, there was little else to catch the observer's eye.

As it became apparent that Ford was **catching up** with its backlog, always the optimists, the slogan "Ford's out front" was adopted for their promotional catalogs.

For the 1947 selling season, Ford then adopted the slogan "Ford's Out Front" in addition to "There's a Ford in your future". "Out front" where? According to the catalog, in style, in beauty, and in performance.

Fog lights are an accessory.

In 1947 Ford continued to produce the sedans of the line in large numbers. There was little left to say about them; Ford's all-steel body was referred to as a "Lifeguard" body, (a word that was to be revived later on in 1956), and during the year the six cylinder engine was upped to 95 hp. Basically though, the car, but for some few styling revisions continued essentially unchanged.

1947 Type 70-B Super De Luxe Tudor sedan   Mr. Paul Reynolds, El Cajon, California

Grill guards have been re-styled (page 33), and horizontal bars of the grill have lost their earlier indented groove.

Resembling the 1946 front end, the most significant difference in the 1947-8 style is the re-placement of the parking lights from their former position between the headlights.

The hood side trim strips appear both as partially grooved design (below) and smooth (right) style which appeared as a running change during 1947.

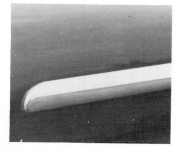

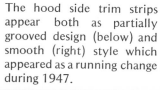

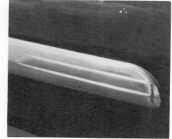

Headlight and parking light rims are smooth rather than the grooved style of 1946.

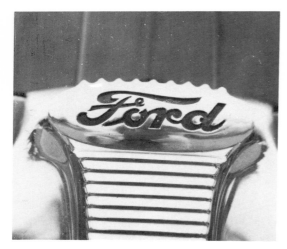

Upper center grill trim has undergone a redesign. Note horizontal grooves beneath script as opposed to 1946 style.

This ornament appears on the Super De Luxe models only with an appropriate 6 or 8.

A two-piece hood ornament includes a chromed metal housing and a transparent plastic insert.

Ford script has been omitted from bumper, rear end trim simplified, and bumper guards re-styled. Back up lights are an accessory.

This trim strip with Ford name replaces the two grooved horizontal strips of 1946.

Rear deck lid handle is unchanged. Note the license plate light incorporated at the top.

Rear fenders are fitted with rubber gravel guards. Note striping of wheels which ended in 1948.

The tail light assembly and fuel filler access flap is unchanged from 1946.

Bumper guards have been re-styled (see page 35) and are now more rounded. Single exhaust pipe is shown here with an accessory chromed tail pipe exhaust deflecter.

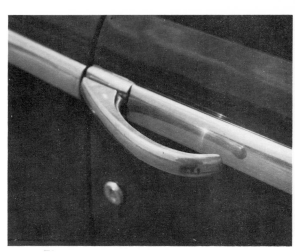

The gracefully curved outside door handle is less ornate than the 1946 style (page 40).

The crank out ventilator is noticibly changed by the elimination, in the 1947 model of the framing trim strip that was used on the 1946 models. (page 41) A new inside locking handle has been added to the vents. (right)

The rear quarter windows in the Tudor sedan can be opened for ventilation by sliding them backwards slightly (far left). Reversing the cranking direction, the glass closes completely and then lowers (near left) or can be lowered completely as shown above.

Accessory radio antennas are mounted on the cowl, or less frequently, the roof of the sedans.

Super De Luxe series closed cars are provided with two pillar lights. A switch (far right) on the right side operates both lamps. De Luxe series do not have a lamp on the left pillar.

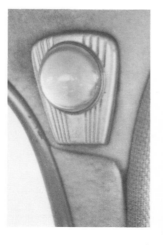

Two rear ash trays are provided in the interior quarter panels of the Super De Luxe Tudor sedan.

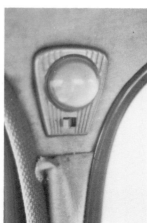

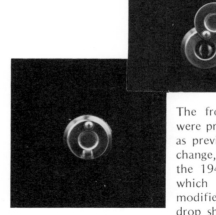

The front doors of all cars were provided with key locks as previously. Late in 1947 a change, often associated with the 1948 model occurred in which the lock's cover was modified to provide a teardrop shaped embossment for easier displacement.

The speedometer has light background highlighted in gold and black and is far more legible than the 1946 style.

The steering wheel is furnished with a horn ring on Super De Luxe series which is omitted in the De Luxe cars.

A tan plastic knob is placed on the shift lever. Design, like that of the horn button (right) is unchanged).

Inside door and window riser handles are unchanged from 1946 with tan plastic knobs and escutcheon plates.

After having been mounted under the dashboard on the firewall since 1932, the voltage dropping resistor has been placed under the hood and mounted on the ignition coil.

A modern leather steering wheel mitten is installed on steering wheel.

Two large dials (speedometer and clock) serve to nicely balance the 1947 dashboard around the radio speaker grill.

The Speedometer is centered directly in front of the steering wheel.

The bright metal rim on glove box door bears Ford Script and, as appropriate, either an "8" or a "6" at the other end.

1947-8

The Adjust-O-Matic Radio continues into 1947 with the touch-bar tuning, but the omission of a remote foot control.

The optional electric clock matches the speedometer in size and style and, as are all of the instruments, it is edge-lighted for improved visibility.

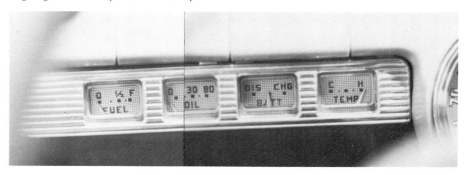

Four gauges are placed directly to the left of the speedometer where they are easily seen by the driver. The faces of these gauges are styled to match clock and speedometer.

An illuminated keyhole for ignition lock and associated steering wheel lock is last used in 1948 when it was discontinued.

Suspended beneath the left corner of the dashboard is the hand brake lever with a built-in trigger release, and the hood latch release knob. Note starter button mounted just above hood release.

A popular accessory is the Columbia two-speed rear axle, a vacuum-operated overdrive unit. Control switch placed between light switch and throttle is for remote electric control of the vacuum solenoid. A feature of the Columbia is a two-speed gearbox placed in the speedometer drive cable to make necessary speed corrections.

Three coupes were offered again in 1947, two with an extended passenger compartment. The most popular was the Sedan Coupe which featured the appearance of a coupe with interior seating for five passengers. The Business coupe was similar but the rear seat was omitted. In addition to these two, a third, relatively rare model was the De Luxe Coupe which was a three passenger coupe **without** the large space behind the front seat.

1947 Type 72-B Super De Luxe Sedan Coupe

Mr. Charles Mackintosh, Carlsbad, California

The doors on the Sedan Coupe and the Business Coupe are wider than those on the De Luxe Coupe to allow for the similarly shaped, but longer, passenger compartment.

The quarter window on the Sedan Coupe opened by pivoting outward at the rear. A chromed inside latch was provided. The same window in the Business Coupe or the De Luxe Coupe did not open.

Arm rests and ash trays are provided for the rear seat passengers of the Sedan Coupe.

The familiar "dove tail" latch (below) with its associated guide and the retracting latch (above) of the pre-war cars is continued through this series.

A smooth, wider lower trim part is used on the 1947-8 models as opposed to the formed part (page 45) employed in 1946.

Unlike the 1946 style, the lower trim continues forward on the front fenders.

1946 shown for comparison

The Super De Luxe Convertible Club Coupe continued to be the most popular and eagerly sought of the whole line. It was a youthful, appealing, car with a "dash" that made it easily the envy of all others.

1947 Type 76 Super De Luxe Convertible Club Coupe

Mr. Carl Burnett, San Diego, California

Above the rear view mirror in the Convertible and the Sportsman is one of three chromed latches which must be manually released or secured.

At the front corners over the windshield of the Convertible and the Sportsman are matching chromed latches.

The Automatic motor-lift (hydraulic) tops of the Convertible and the Sportsman are operated on command from this control knob mounted below the light- and the throttle-knobs under the dashboard.

The ventilator windows of the Convertible (and closed cars) open manually. The window crank is secured to the shaft with a screw. An escutcheon plate behind the crank matches that on the window riser handle.

Continued in 1947 after its 1946 introduction is the Sportsman Coupe, basically a Convertible Club Sedan dressed up with a wooden body patterned on the Station Wagon construction. The car was fitted with special appointments including standard hydraulically operated window lifts. It did not attain the popularity that was predicted for the model though and was discontinued late in 1947.

1947 Type 71 Sportsman

Mr. Robert McCoppin, Hayward, California

Forward portion of car is identical with the others in the year except for the addition of "Sportsman" script at hood sides.

Outside door handles are same as on Station Wagons (page 46).

The quarter window rotates to open, and like the front door windows is hydraulically operated on the Sportsman.

Standard keylock is built into each door.

The lower edge of the door panels and body quarter section are curved outwards over the enclosed running boards similar to sedans. Below the curve is a chromed trim strip.

These snap fasteners assist in keeping the inside snug and quiet.

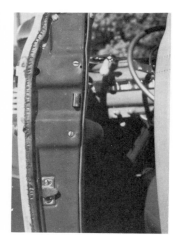

The door lock and dovetail guide are same as sedans.

A chromed trim strip is installed at the corners of the deck lid and hides a seam, not a joint as seen in the foreground.

The "Sportsman" script appears again in the right rear corner on the deck lid.

A unique tail lamp is provided (compare page 53) due to the wider overhang of the Sportsman body.

Four matching bumper guards are standard for all models.

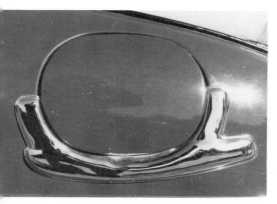

An accessory chrome trim dresses up the fuel filler access flap.

The spare wheel is secured flat on the rear deck although in other models this year it is mounted in a vertical position against the rear "wall".

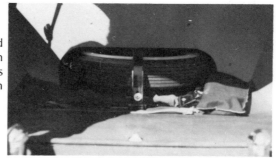

FORD   FORD CUSTOM

The previous designations were dropped with the introduction of the new model, and now "Ford" and "Ford Custom" lines were adopted in place of the former "De Luxe" and "Super De Luxe" respectively.

BODY TYPES

70 A	Ford Tudor Sedan	73 A	Ford Fordor Sedan
70 B	Ford Custom Tudor Sedan	73 B	Ford Custom Fordor Sedan
72 A	Ford Club Coupe	76 B	Ford Custom Convertible Coupe
72 B	Ford Custom Club Coupe	79	Ford Custom Station Wagon
72 C	Ford Business Coupe		

SPECIFICATIONS

"Lifeguard" Body. The '49 Ford's new, rigid "Lifeguard" Body provides new security, with all-steel, welded, full-arch bridge construction. Body is bolted to frame at 22 points, to form a strong, solid unit. Overall height from road: 62.8 inches. Overall length: 196.8 inches. Width: 71.7 inches.

5 Cross Member, Box Section Frame, of completely new double-drop design, makes possible lower center of gravity; better roadability. 4" x 3¾" box-section siderails, with continuous weld from front suspension cross member to back of rear axle. 5 husky cross members provide twist-resistant lateral bracing.

New Suspension System. Independently suspended front wheels have "Hydra-Coil" Front Springs which combine soft acting coil springs with double-action, air-craft-type hydraulic shock absorbers. Extra-long, extra-strong "Para-Flex" Rear Springs of leaf design are mounted parallel to frame. New inserts between leaves, and rubber bushings at shackles and brackets make lubrication unnecessary. Aircraft-type double-action, hydraulic shock absorbers at rear.

New symmetrical steering linkage keeps the new Ford "on track" at a finger touch. Steering ease, security and roadability greatly increased.

New "Magic Action" King-Size Brakes. In forward or reverse motion, the new Ford's duo-servo, self-energizing brakes use car momentum to increase pressure of brake linings on drums; up to 35% easier to apply by actual test; mean easier, safer straight-line stops.

Hypoid Rear Axle means quieter operation and longer gear life . . . minimizes tunnel height in rear floor. Extra-strong, lightweight banjo-type housing gives greater service accessibility.

Hotchkiss Drive transmits all driving and braking forces through "Para-Flex" Rear Springs for smoother, more comfortable starts and stops. Hotchkiss Drive reduces unsprung weight; makes possible softer, more flexible engine mounting for greater smoothness.

Your Choice of Power. New 100 h.p. V-8—new 95 h.p. Six. Both have new combustion chambers for high-compression performance with non-premium gasoline. Both have "Deep Breath" Manifolding . . . "Equa-Flo" Cooling . . . new lubrication system. Both have new positive crankcase ventilation . . . new, exclusive "Loadomatic" ignition for accurate spark advance under all conditions . . . 4-ring, oil-saving, aluminum pistons . . . Ford cast alloy crankshaft . . . top-mounted accessories for easy servicing . . . easy-acting semi-centrifugal clutch. V-8, bore: 3³⁄₁₆ inches, stroke: 3¾ inches. Six, bore: 3.3 inches, stroke: 4.4 inches. Up to 10% more miles per gallon of gas.

New Overdrive, optional at extra cost, acts as an automatic "fourth gear" that cuts engine speed, saves plenty on gasoline, means greater driving ease and longer engine life.

"Mid Ship" Ride. You ride between the wheels, in the level center section of the '49 Ford's "lounge car" interior, where the going's smoothest. Seats are deep, soft, sofa comfortable, with ample hip and shoulder room for 3 on each. Front seat 57" wide—rear seat 60". Front seat adjustable through 4¼ inch range.

Special seat construction minimizes waste space, increases touring comfort. New appointments and furnishings throughout.

"Picture Window" Visibility. More than 20 square feet of window area in Tudor Sedans. Rear window alone is 88% larger. Narrow corner posts and body center pillars increase all-around "see-ability."

New Instrument Panel groups all control indicators and speedometer directly in front of driver in single large cluster for "at-a-glance" reading through new two-spoke steering wheel. All instruments illuminated by soft, non-glare "black light." Windshield wiper control, starter button and all other controls located in easy reach on panel. Ample glove compartment.

New Hardware. Exterior door handles are pull-out type; open doors effortlessly and surely. Interior handles specially designed so they can't snag clothing. Doors cannot open by accident, because interior handles pull up to open. Locks return to unlocked position when doors close—keys can't be locked in. Ignition key unlocks either front door, even when locked from inside.

"Magic Air" Temperature Control, optional at extra cost, lets you choose your own climate the year 'round. In summer, plenty of fresh, cooling outside air . . . in winter, a wealth of clean, warm air circulated without drafts through the car.

Two Series . . . Six Models. Ford Custom: Tudor Sedan, Fordor Sedan, Club Coupe, Convertible Club Coupe, Station Wagon. Ford: Tudor Sedan, Fordor Sedan, Club Coupe, Business Coupe.

10 Baked Enamel Colors.
    Black • Sea-mist Green • Colony Blue • Midland Maroon Metallic • *Bayview Blue Metallic • Arabian Green • Birch Gray **Miami Cream • *Gun-metal Gray Metallic • **Fez Red.
  *Custom models only. Station Wagon not available in Gun-metal Gray Metallic.
  **Convertible Club Coupe only.

Your choice of fine upholstery: Custom Sedans and Club Coupe upholstered in either blue-gray tweed broadcloth, or gray-green stripe mohair. Tan leather upholstery at extra cost.

Ford Sedans and Business Coupe upholstered in green stripe broadcloth or green and red stripe mohair, tan leather at extra cost.

Station Wagon driver's seat upholstered with genuine leather, passenger seats with vinyl.

Convertible Club Coupe upholstered with combination of genuine leather and bedford cord in colors to harmonize with body exteriors. Upholstery combinations include red leather with beige bedford cord, tan leather with beige bedford cord and green leather with green bedford cord.

Wheels and Tires: Wide-base full drop-center rims on ventilated steel disc wheels. New 7.10 x 15 6-ply low pressure tires standard on Station Wagon, 6.00 x 16 4-ply standard on other models . . . 6.00 x 16 6-ply and new 6.70 x 15 4- or 6-ply low pressure tires available at extra cost on all models except Station Wagon . . . White sidewall tires optional at extra cost.

*1949 saw the introduction of the first new Ford passenger car to be presented since the death of Henry Ford in April of 1947. Aside from its obvious change in appearance, the car had a new suspension system incorporating independent front coil springs and longitudinal rear springs in the rear coupled with tubular hydraulic shock absorbers. While in itself not terribly remarkable, this change was the **first** departure from the transverse leaf spring system first installed by Henry Ford in his 1906 Model N!*

Visibility was increased by the use of larger windows (the rear window alone was 137 square inches longer), brakes were improved to offer "an up to 35% easier to apply system", and a new symetrical steering system was provided. Little-noticed at the time was the claimed "Life-Guard" body and frame structure.

*Although much earlier, Fords had been available with Columbia two-speed axles, this accessory was doomed with the introduction of a factory-installed two-speed auxiliary transmission (Overdrive) mounted directly behind the conventional transmission in the driveline. This popular optional accessory provides a "fourth gear" by **automatically** shifting self-contained gears to reduce the engine-to-rear-end ratio and thus reduce engine speed for on-the-road economy. With Overdrive it is not at all unusual to obtain 24-26 miles per gallon against a typical 18 for conventional drive.*

*The styling changes which repositioned the passengers between the axles, described as "Mid-Ship" ride, also virtually eliminated the outlines of the fenders, and a somewhat flat-sided appearance resulted which has essentially remained ever since. As mild-appearing as the style change may now appear, it was, for the time, a **significant** change, one so abrupt that it earned the 1949 model the designation "The Car of the Year."*

1949

The Coupe body style became available in three types which included the Ford coupe, the Ford Custom Coupe, and the Ford Business Coupe which omitted the rear seat found in the other two.

A completely redesigned front end introduced the cyclops-like center ornament.

1949 Type 72 B Ford Custom Club Coupe

Mr. E. C. Maxwell, Escondido, California

Back up lights, righthand mirror, and spotlight are accessories.

The Ford Custom line is identified on the 1949 by this trim plate at the forward end of the side trim stripes.

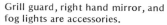
Grill guard, right hand mirror, and fog lights are accessories.

Frontal features of the 1949 model are immediately identified by the single "spinner" at the center and the word FORD above it.

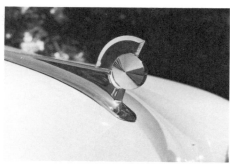

A modern chrome-and-plastic hood ornament makes its appearance this year.

Headlight rims continue to be plain, not grooved, but are wider than the previous year style.

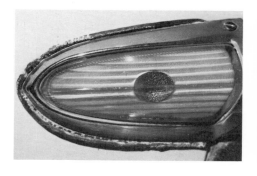

Parking lights are incorporated in the flowing design of the radiator center grill strip.

The "spinner" bears an "8" or a "6" as appropriate and designates the engine choice.

Chromed block letters form the word at the front of the hood.

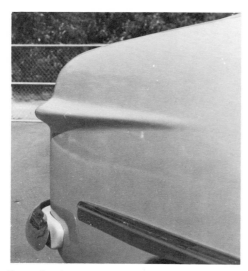

Rear fenders are pressed to form a decorative, but not necessarily functional section.

The windshield of the new 1949 car resembles the earlier style but does not interchange.

The absence of definitive fender lines is clearly seen in this view of the 1949 rear quarter.

Bumper guards are again restyled. Two on the front and two on the rear bumpers are standard, not optional accessories.

White side wall tires are an optional extra. 6.00 x 16 tires are standard (7.10 x 15 on the Station Wagon). Low pressure 6.70 x 15 tires and 15 inch wheels are an optional extra cost accessory this year.

The ventilator pane is now shaped more acutely due to the added sweep-back of the windshield corner post. Compare with earlier style on page 54.

A pressed-steel hinge is used as the upper pivot of the vent window.

New this year are pull-out door handles and a new style of keylock.

The rear quarter window of the Ford Club Coupe and the Ford Custom Club Coupe can be pivoted open for added ventilation. The feature is omitted on the Ford Business Coupe.

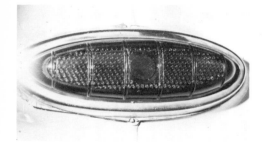

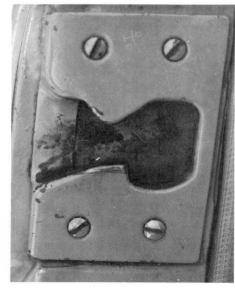

A new door lock featuring a rotary latch appears on the doors of the 1949 models.

The external fuel filler cap returns this year, and tail lights are placed in a horizontal position to emphasize the formed flare in the fender.

Smooth, chromed, deck lid hinges are featured in 1949.

The one-piece rear window is said to be 88% larger than the previous model.

The rear deck lid handle is concealed in this decorative trim piece which also contains a license plate light.

The steering wheel in the Ford Custom line was fitted with a horn ring (omitted in the Ford line).

The dashboard in the 1949 Station Wagon (shown) is wood grained. Other models had painted dashboards.

The starter switch, light switch and windshield wiper controls are placed to the left of the steering column. The grooved trim strips (also at right) are used only on the 1949 dashboard.

To the right of the steering column are the ignition lock, choke knob, and cigarette lighter. The globe-shaped chromed control knobs are new this year.

The hood release knob is now chromed to match the other control knobs on the dash-board.

The cowl visor has been omitted, but two air ducts bring outside air into the passenger compartment, and butterfly valves in the ducts are controlled by a pair of knobs at the bottom of the dashboard on either side of the steering column.

The instruments are contained within the speedometer housing and are grouped neatly around it for maximum clarity. Although turn signals were an optional accessory, all speedometers were prepared for the possible installation by containing the necessary indicator lamp housings near the bottom. Illumination of the cluster was by "black-lighting" which produced a spectacular display of glowing dials and pointers in complete darkness, but was unsatisfactory in normal ambient lighting situations.

A black-faced clock is set into the dashboard near the top center for maximum visibility by all passengers.

Two heaters were offered, the one shown here which merely heated and recirculated the air within the passenger compartment, and the Magic Air unit (preceeding page) which also optionally accepted fresh air through the ventilating air ducts as well.

A round tan plastic ball replaces the pear-shaped gear shift lever knob of the 1948 model (page 56).

A five push-button "Hi Fidelity" radio is offered for the first time. The speaker for the radio is mounted beneath the plastic grill set in the top of the dashboard (right). Since the windshield wiper control knob has been relocated to the dashboard (page 73), there is no longer a knob at the base of the windshield.

The control knob for the optional Overdrive transmission is located beneath the dashboard between the light and the windshield wiper control knobs.

The gray-green stripe mohair upholstery shown here is one of three choices available in the Custom Sedans and Club Coupe. (The others were blue-gray tweed broadcloth or, at extra cost, tan leather.) Station Wagons were done with tan leather on the front seat, and, for the first time, matching vinyl on the passenger seats.

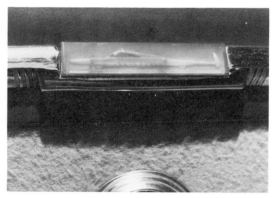

Although greatly resembling an airplane, this plastic insignia on the door sills was to represent a modernistic automobile.

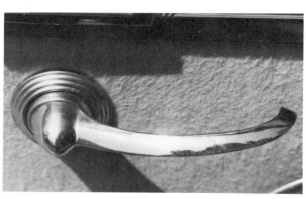

Safety inside door handles require an upward pull to open, and a new shape is used for these handles. A modern "spinner" hub appears at the center behind which is a chromed, grooved escutcheon plate. The window riser crank handle is fitted with a metal ball similar to the dashboard control knobs.

Closed cars are fitted with these garment hangers over the quarter windows.

A restyled pillar lamp is installed on both pillars of the Ford Custom De Luxe models. Ford De Luxe sedans and Ford De Luxe business coupe however, only have one light on the left side. A switch on the instrument panel operate the lamps, and in addition, on the Ford Custom De Luxe models, switches in the cowl turn the lights on when either door is opened.

An ashtray is placed in the instrument panel.

An optional hot-water heater installed on the firewall is controlled by switches suspended beneath the instrument panel. Left switch controls blower motor, right hand one the temperature.

The Tudor sedans are nearly symetrical around the sturdy looking window post.

The rear window has been enlarged from the previous style (page 53) by a claimed 137 square inches.

Doors on the Tudor sedans are narrower by several inches than those on the Coupes.

Ventilator panes now appear in the rear quarter windows of the sedans.

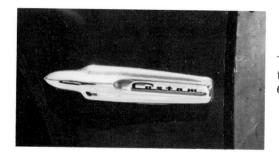

The identification plate on the Station Wagon differs from the Ford Custom plate on other models (page 68).

1949 Type 79 Ford Custom Station Wagon

Mr. Paul Vorweck, Laguna Beach, California

Entirely new this year is the two-door wooden body station wagon replacing the long-established four door model of past years.

As with other models, the vent windows in the Station Wagon pivot open. The track at the rear edge is fixed and does not lower with the window in the door.

A single wide door opens to give good access to the rear seats.

Sliding rear quarter windows are provided for ventilation. Note that the hardwood panels actually are supported by a steel framework for added safety.

The pull-out door handle design is adapted to the Station Wagon, but is not identical with the handles on the other models.

From the front the Station Wagon rightly appears to be identical with the other cars in the line as it shares most parts forward of the cowl.

The wooden structure of the Station Wagon is framed in an all-steel supporting structure.

The spare wheel is carried in a two-piece painted cover at the rear. Tire size is 7.10 x 15.

The tail lamp is hinged with a pantograph arrangement to hold it facing rearward regardless of position of the tail gate.

A folding hinge at either side supports the tail gate securely when lowered for loading.

For all models in 1949, the fuel filler pipe extends through the left rear finder. On the station wagon it appears on the corner post.

The two-pane rear window has lost its rectangular appearance for a more modern effect, and its frame now fits gracefully into the steel roof lines.

Opened, the rear window, or "lift gate", provides increased ventilation through the passenger compartment

With tail gate lowered, and lift gate raised, a maximum access is obtained for the loading of bulky objects.

A locking handle secures the two rear sections.

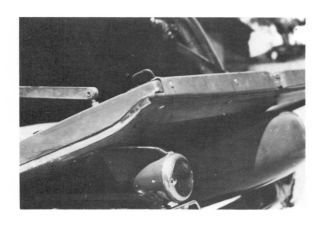

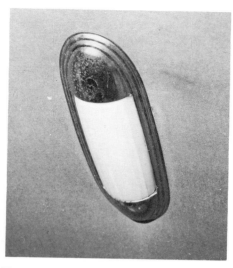

The dome light of the Station Wagon differs from the pillar lights installed in the closed cars (page 77).

This switch, mounted on the right-hand window pillar controls the Station Wagon dome light.

Two ash trays are provided, one at each side of the center seat.

The second seat is split at the center to allow added access to the rear. Both the second and the third seat are upholstered in tan vinyl although the drivers seat is done in full leather. Either or both of the two rear seats can be removed for increased cargo space.

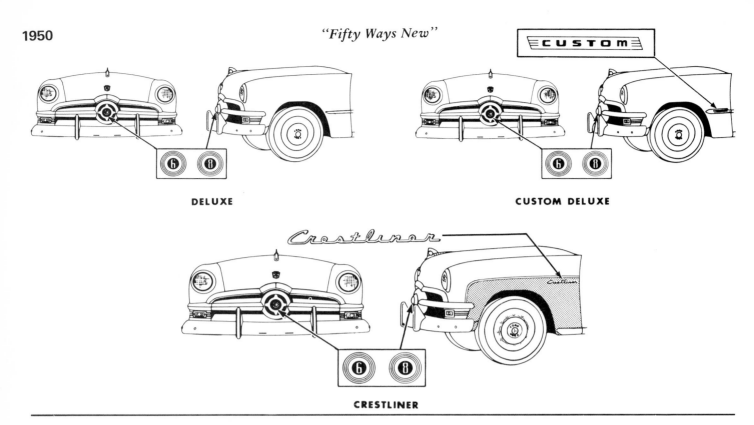

DELUXE   CUSTOM DELUXE

CRESTLINER

BODY TYPES

In 1950, "Ford" became "Deluxe" and the "Ford Custom" line became the "Custom Deluxe".

70 A Deluxe Tudor Sedan		73 A Deluxe Fordor Sedan
70 B Custom deluxe Tudor sedan		73 B Custom Deluxe Fordor Sedan
72 A Deluxe Club Coupe		76 B Custom Deluxe Convertible Coupe
72 B Custom Deluxe Club Coupe		79 Custom Deluxe Station Wagon
72 C Deluxe Business Coupe		70 C Crestliner

SPECIFICATIONS:

V-8 ENGINE: 100 brake h.p.; $3\frac{3}{16}$" bore, $3\frac{3}{4}$" stroke; 32.5 taxable h.p.; "Equa-Poise" mounting; 4-ring, tin-plated, aluminum alloy pistons with steel struts; new cam design; laminated composition material timing gear; "Loadomatic" ignition.

FULL-PRESSURE LUBRICATION: crankcase capacity, 4 qts. normal refill, 5 when filter element replaced; oil filter at extra cost; helical gear oil pump; directed-flow crankcase ventilation.

FUEL SYSTEM: capacity, 19 gal. on Station Wagon, 16 on other models; oil bath air cleaner at extra cost; dual downdraft carburetor; automatic heat control valve.

"EQUA-FLO" COOLING SYSTEM: capacity 21 qts.; 22 with heater; full-length water jackets surround each cylinder completely; balanced-type thermostats and recirculation by-passes; dual water pumps; unique 3-blade fan; pressure-type radiator cap.

CLUTCH AND TRANSMISSION: semi-centrifugal type clutch; 3-speed helical gear transmission with synchronizers for second and third speeds.

AUTOMATIC OVERDRIVE: optional at extra cost; cuts in at 27 mph (approx.); cuts out at 21 mph (approx.); ratio 0.70 to 1.

DOUBLE-DROP FRAME: box-section side rails and 5 cross members. Convertible and Station Wagon frames specially reinforced.

INDEPENDENT FRONT WHEEL SUSPENSION: swinging link type with coil springs, double-acting, tubular, hydraulic shock absorbers and new, one-piece, rubber-mounted stabilizer.

REAR SUSPENSION: semi-elliptic leaf springs, longitudinally mounted; rubber bushings in shackles and brackets and impregnated inserts between tips of upper leaves eliminate need for lubrication; double-acting, tubular, hydraulic shock absorbers.

REAR AXLE: semi-floating type; hypoid gears. Gear ratios without Overdrive: 3.91 to 1 standard, 4.27 to 1 optional on Station Wagon; all other models 3.73 to 1 standard, 4.10 to 1 optional. Gear ratios with Overdrive: Station Wagon 4.27 to 1; other models 4.10 to 1.

"MAGIC ACTION" HYDRAULIC BRAKES: 4-wheel duo-servo type; composite steel and cast iron drums; molded linings; lining area, 182.5 sq. in. on Station Wagon, 176 sq. in. on other models. Rear service brakes, actuated by dash-mounted T-handle, serve as parking brake.

SYMMETRICAL STEERING LINKAGE: worm and roller steering gear with needle-bearing mounted, triple-tooth roller; gear ratio, 17.7 to 1; over-all steering ratio, 23.2 to 1; 18" diameter, 2-spoke steering wheel.

WHEELS AND TIRES: 6.00 x 16 4-ply tires on $4\frac{1}{2}$" rims standard on Deluxe models; 6.70 x 15 4-ply tires on 5" rims standard on Custom Deluxe models except Station Wagon; 7.10 x 15 6-ply tires on 5" rims standard on Station Wagon. 6.70 x 15 4-ply tires on 5" rims optional at extra cost for Deluxe models. Standard tires have black sidewalls. All tires available with white sidewalls at extra cost.

EXTERIOR DIMENSIONS: 114" wheelbase; 56" tread, front and rear (Station Wagon rear 60"); over-all length 196.7" (Station Wagon 208").

INSTRUMENTS AND CONTROLS: Fuel level, oil pressure, battery charge and water temperature indicators grouped around speedometer in single cluster. Starter push-button; combination exterior light and instrument panel light switch; interior light switch; windshield wiper control; ventilating duct controls; T-handle controls for hood latch and parking brake; finger-tip gear shift lever; head lamp beam control switch;

rubber-padded clutch and brake pedals; treadle-type accelerator pedal.

1950 FORD V-8 LINE: Tudor Sedan, Fordor Sedan and Business Coupe in Deluxe models; Tudor Sedan, Fordor Sedan, Club Coupe, Convertible Club Coupe and Station Wagon in Custom Deluxe Models.

11 BODY COLORS: Cambridge Maroon Metallic, Sheridan Blue, Sunland Beige, Palisade Green, Dover Gray and Black for all models; Bimini Blue Metallic, Osage Green Metallic, and Hawthorne Green Metallic for Custom Deluxe models only. Matador Red Metallic and Sportsman's Green for Convertible only.

DELUXE EQUIPMENT: Dual windshield wipers, twin horns, one sun visor, rear view mirror, ash tray and glove compartment in instrument panel; foam rubber pad in front seat cushion; mohair or broadcloth upholstery; interior light on left center pillar with switch on instrument panel.

CUSTOM DELUXE EQUIPMENT: (In addition to or in place of items listed for Deluxe models). Horn ring and Custom Deluxe horn button; two sun visors; locking glove compartment door; chrome finials on instrument panel; cigar lighter, electric clock (at extra cost); chrome exterior reveal molding at windshield on all models and at rear window of Sedans and Club Coupe; wheel trim rings (at extra cost); one ash tray in rear compartment of Fordor, 2 in other models; two assist straps in Tudor and Club Coupe; robe cord in Fordor. Extra-quality mohair or broadcloth upholstery in hard-top models; seven leather or leather and bedford cord upholstery combinations for Convertible; genuine leather on driver's seat, vinyl on passenger seats in Station Wagon; two interior lights (one in Convertible and Station Wagon) operated automatically by either front door or by manual switch; arm rests on both front doors; arm rests at both sides of rear seats (except Convertible and Station Wagon).

When the 1950 Model was presented, it appeared to have many features that were not included in the 1949, but possibly quite a few of them were items that had only been delayed on the earlier model. For example, 1950 eliminated the protruding gas filler and the pull-out door locks. Other changes were normal re-stylings of such items as the hood ornament, the front end trim and parking lights.

A notable item was the introduction of the Ford Crest on the 1950 models, an item which has since become synonymous with the Ford Motor Company. First employed on the hood and rear deck of the 1950 models, it has persisted on various forms and applications to the present.

Among the 50 (or more) changes claimed for the 1950 Ford were some that were of some significance i.e. the new engines for 1950 were fitted with 3-bladed fans (and smaller driving pulleys) to reduce the noise, new pistons built to control expansion and reduce "slap", and a new, quieter camshaft, and some that were **not** so significant (as might be expected) such as a new double-walled glove compartment door hinge!

1950 Type 70 B Custom Deluxe Tudor sedan

Mr. Peter Doughtie, Oceanside, California

1950

1950 Type 76 B Custom Deluxe Convertible Club Coupe

Accessories on this car include dual spotlights, wheel trim rings, rear fender shields, front fender trim, outside rear view mirrors, and non-Ford instrument panel dress-up trim.

Mr. Howard Lampke, Orange, California

Ford claimed that the 1950 Tudor sedans had the most "hip and shoulder room of any car in the low-price field" and claimed room for six big people. With new non-sag front seat springs and foam rubber cushioning, they were probably not exagerating the comfort provided in the Tudor sedan.

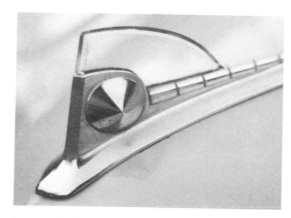

A new plastic and chrome hood ornament appears this year. Similar to 1949, (pg. 69), it has a longer plastic fin.

Identical with the 1949 part, the radiator grill ornament bears the designation of the engine selection in the car.

The same plain chromed headlamp door is used again in 1950, as was employed in 1949.

1950 saw the introduction of the Ford Crest and it appears here on the center of the hood at the front. It also appears on the deck lid (page 92).

Parking lamps have been recessed into the fender under a chromed trim strip where they are protected by the wrapped-around bumper.

The chromed windshield trim of the Custom Deluxe series is omitted on the lower-priced Deluxe cars.

Dual windshield wipers are provided with both arms operated through a linkage from a single vacuum motor under the cowl.

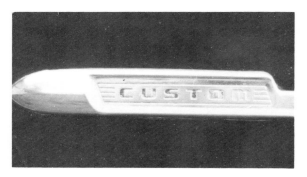

The Custom Deluxe line cars are identified by this insignia which appears on the front fenders. Deluxe cars have a plain trim strip.

A 35" long, chromed center strip is installed to dress up the hoods of both the 1949 and the 1950 models.

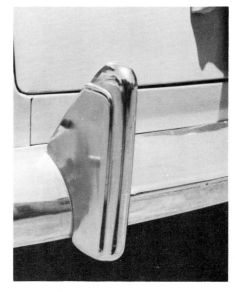

Again in 1949 the bumper guards are re-styled, and are furnished as standard parts, not optional accessories.

The escutcheon behind the inside door handle (and window riser crank) on the Super Deluxe line is chromed metal.

The inside handles on the Deluxe series are identical with those on the Custom Deluxe, but the escutcheon plates are tan plastic rather than chromed (right).

A new rotary door latch replaces the 1949 style which was used only one year and then abandoned as unsatisfactory.

The same futuristic automobile insignia is employed again on the door sill above the handle. For safety, handles must be rotated upwards to release the door latch.

A new outside door handle featuring a push-button release replaces the pull-out style used last year.

The rear fender continues to have a definite bulge for decorative effect.

The fuel filler pipe has again retreated beneath the access flap in the left rear fender after appearing externally on the 1949 models.

The new Ford Crest appears on th rear deck lid.

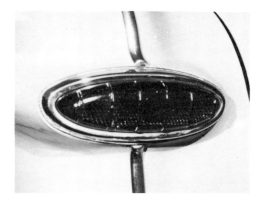

The rear lamps are unchanged. 1949 and 1950 were identical. The chromed welting at the fender parting seam in the photo at right is an accessory dress up item.

The gear shift knob is the same as 1949.

The "flat" gray plastic steering wheel continues in 1950 and is unchanged from 1949 except for that on the Convertible (below) which is black. The turn signal is an optional accessory.

The Custom Deluxe models are furnished with a horn ring and a special "Custom Deluxe horn button" (below right).

The Custom Deluxe Convertible Club Coupe was equipped with a black steering wheel and gear shift knob among its other special appointments.

The radio speaker grill continues to be placed at the top center of the instrument panel.

This is the optional Custom seven tube-plus-rectifier radio which also features an "on" function incorporated in each push button and "off" at the left button. The tone control also shows an indication at the center of the dial ranging from "lo noise" to "music".

The other of the two available radios for 1950 is the Deluxe set which has five tubes-plus-rectifier. The on/off switch is incorporated in the volume control.

A view of the Convertible Coupe is emphasized by its exclusive use of a black steering wheel and gear shift knob.

The electric clock is an optional accessory which is generally found in Custom Deluxe cars.

The "Magic Air" control unit is mounted under the instrument panel just to the right of the steering column. This optional accessory combines incoming fresh air with recirculating air for heating and defrosting purposes. A self-contained light illuminates the dial at night.

The speedometer includes provision for the optional turn signals, and is essentially identical with the 1949 unit. "Black lighting" persisted, as a means of illuminating the instruments at night, but was abandoned later due to an unsatisfactorily low level of illumination in normal ambient situations.

At the right side of the instrument panel is a glove compartment. Only the Custom Deluxe line cars were equipped with a lock for this compartment. Likewise, two sun visors are furnished with this line, the De Luxe cars have only one.

The absence of a horn ring is an immediate indication that this car is a Deluxe. Other subtle differences include the escutcheon plates behind the window riser crank.

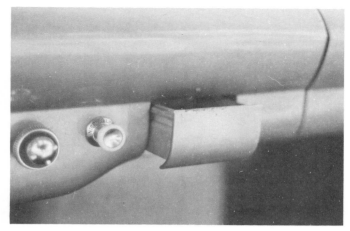

Just to the left of the ash tray is a new control which is the pillar-light switch now appearing on the panel for the first time.

An accessory map light hangs under the instrument panel near the ash tray.

At both ends of the instrument panel on the Custom Deluxe series a chromed trim piece is provided. Below it is the control knob for the optional Overdrive transmission and to the right of that the control for the left-side incoming air.

In their catalogs, Ford called these trim pieces "finials", technically an incorrect designation as the term applies to the *upward-pointing* ornament or cap of a spire.

A re-styled knob, superceding the ball-shaped control knobs of 1949 makes its first appearance in the 1950 cars.

During 1950, in order to boost lagging sales, Ford introduced a "new" model called the Crestliner. Basically a Tudor sedan with special trim, the car was conspicuous by the wide sweeping trim applied to its sides. Overlooked is the fact that this was the **first** factory application of vinyl to the roofs of steel-topped cars, a practice that was to be used for only about a year and then discontinued, not again to be revived until some twelve years later.

1950 Type 70 C Crestliner

Mr. Robert Kennedy, Whittier, California

In a folder dated July of 1950, The Crestliner was described by the factory as "an answer for those who want to combine the smart styling of a fine sports car with the practical advantages and economy of a conventional Ford Tudor Sedan". However, it will be seen that this was wishful thinking, because **that** answer, as attractive as the car may have been, never caught the public's fancy and it was shortly to be replaced.

Available in only two color combinations, (Coronation Red Metallic and Black, and Sportsman's Green and Black), the effect of the airfoils is heightened by the contrast in color.

A specially designed gold-finished Crestliner name-plate appears on the front fenders.

Obviously a Tudor sedan, the effect is nevertheless changed with the addition of the contrasting side trim.

This unique chromed wheel cover with a concentric ring of circles is supplied only with the 1950 Crestliner.

A durable, vinyl decking material is applied over glass-wool padding placed over the steel top of the car and a chromed trim strip installed at the edges. Windows are trimmed with bright metal.

A unique basket-weave design is moulded into the vinyl top covering material.

A seam runs the length of the top on each side.

The fender shields are standard on the dress-up Crestliner.

Chromed windshield mouldings are used and the instrument panel is two-toned to match the exterior and with a black facing surface for hightened drama. Instrument knobs are black with chromed inserts.

A special, *black*, four-spoked steering wheel and horn ring is used on the Crestliner. A similar wheel in brown was available as an extra-cost option on the other models.

The hub of the special Crestliner steering wheel is decorated with a stylized letter "F".

Directly above the standard electric clock, the name "Crestliner" appears in the chromed script.

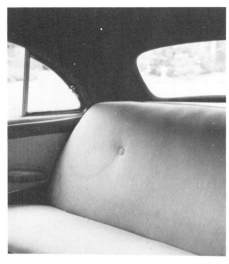

Seat backs and cushions are covered in Bedford Cord pin-striped in color to match the exterior but the facing surfaces are black leather. The headliner is a special black simulated leather material.

Curiously, this particular car was delivered with the "Magic-Air Temperature Control" system, but with no radio. Accordingly, a blanking plate appears on the dashboard where the radio would otherwise have been installed.

1950 Type 73 B Custom Deluxe Fordor sedan

Rear door window is fitted with an adjustable ventilator and the door edge smoothly faired into the rear quarter.

A chromed trim strip runs the entire length of the car just above the rear wheel housing opening.

Type 76 B Custom Deluxe Convertible Coupe   Mr. Doug Henshaw, Orange, California

With windows lowered (and rear flap dropped) the Convertible offers a well-ventilated, sporty appearance. Tops are offered in three colors, Black, tan, or green to harmonize with the body and upholstery choices.

A hydraulic power unit, controlled by a T-handle on the dash, operates the top. When down, the top folds neatly into a well behind the rear seat and a snap-on cover is furnished to fit smoothly over the folded top.

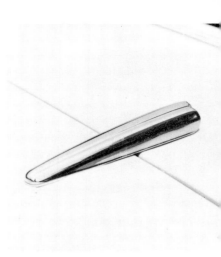

The 1950 rear deck lid handle is almost devoid of chrome. The lid lock is under the flap at the right side of the chromed trim.

A new trunk hinge was introduced in 1950. Seemingly more sturdy, it is not as graceful as the earlier style (page 72).

Front and rear bumper guards are standard, not optional extras. Optional turn indicators, when selected, function by intermittently lighting the stop light circuit within the appropriate tail lamp.

Wheel trim rings, applied over the standard wheel covers, were available at extra cost. This style virtually eliminates the appearance of the wheel itself.

Atop the windshield frame of the Convertible are two locating pins against which the top latching mechanisms bear.

In the rear, ash trays are provided on each side near the quarter window crank handles.

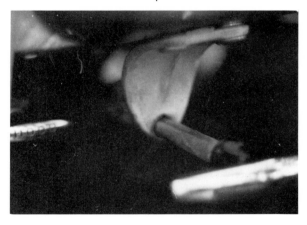

The hood release (below) is a chromed T-head handle placed just to the left of the parking brake handle beneath the instrument panel.

The hood is hinged at the rear and opens from the front.

A mechanical latch under the hood must be manually unlatched after the hood is released by the cable.

1950 Type 76 B Custom Deluxe Convertible Coupe with accessory Continental kit

Mr. Ken Keyser, Walnut Creek, California

The Continental kit is a recurring accessory offered by Dealers and frequently found in other accessory sources. The Ford crest, now omitted from the deck lid, is then placed on the tire cover.

Extenders are used to move the bumper rearwards to provide mounting space for the spare wheel and auxiliary panels, painted to match the car, installed to extend the appearance of the body.

The kit is made to mechanically latch against a latch affixed above the rear deck handle. It is hinged at the lower end for easiest access to the luggage compartment.

1950 Type 76 B Custom Deluxe Convertible Coupe with trim accessories

Mr. Howard Lampke, Orange, California

A chromed instrument panel dress-up trim surrounds the electric clock.

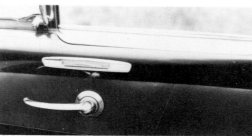

A chromed dress-up window sill trim adds interest at this point.

Chromed fender welting heightens the effect of the parting line.

A genuine Ford accessory is this Front Fender Trim.

1950 Type 72 B Deluxe Club Coupe with accessory Sun Visor   Mr. Paul Vorweck, Laguna Beach, California

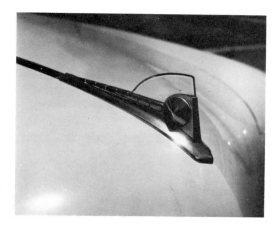

1950 Deluxe Club Coupe, shown here with accessory fender skirts.

The windshield is framed in rubber moulding. Custom Deluxe models had an exposed chrome trim strip in its place.

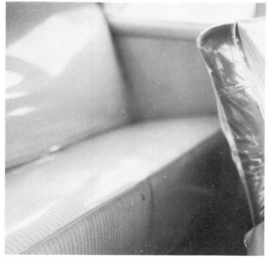

The Club coupes were fitted with a wide, but fairly shallow, rear seat for two additional passengers.

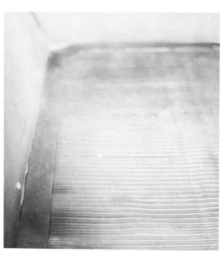

In the Deluxe Business Coupe, the rear seat was omitted, the walls cardboard-trimmed, and the floor furnished with a rubber mat to provide added cargo space.

The outside Windshield Visor is a Ford accessory for 1950. Made of metal, it is painted to match the car.

As with the windshield, the rear window on the Deluxe models is trimmed in rubber rather than bright metal.

The quarter windows on the Coupes do not open.

Compare page 90 for a view of the Custom Deluxe car with metal-trimmed windshield.

Although the trim stripe continues on the sides of the Deluxe series, the insignia bearing the "Custom" identification of the Custom Deluxe series at the front is omitted.

In addition to two pillar lights, the Custom Deluxe sedans and Club Coupe also had two assist straps placed below the lights.

The Deluxe sedans and coupes had only one pillar light, on the left side, and no assist straps.

All closed cars were fitted with garment hangers on each side above the rear quarter windows.

As an example of "running" changes made in a specific model, note the scissors-type deck lid catch on a 1950 Convertible at the left, and the same catch, now a latching mechanism, on the one at the right.

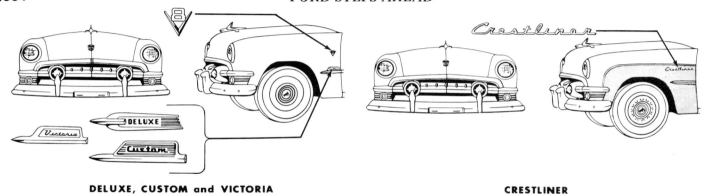

DELUXE, CUSTOM and VICTORIA   CRESTLINER

Again in 1951, a name change. The former Custom Deluxe series becomes the "Custom" line but the lower priced Deluxe series retains its name. 1951 also saw the introduction of the soon-to-be-well-known name "Country Squire".

BODY TYPES

60 Victoria	72 C Deluxe Business Coupe
70 A Deluxe Tudor Sedan	73 A Deluxe Fordor Sedan
70 B Custom Tudor Sedan	73 B Custom Fordor Sedan
70 C Crestliner	76 Custom Convertible Coupe
72 B Custom Club Coupe	79 Custom "Country Squire" Station Wagon

SPECIFICATIONS:

V-8 ENGINE: 100 brake h.p.; 3.1875 in. bore, 3.75 in. stroke; 32.5 taxable h.p.; "Power Dome" combustion chambers; tin-plated Super-Fitted aluminum pistons, offset pins, 4 rings with chrome-plated top ring; "Rota-Quiet" valves; Quiet-Contoured camshaft; "Silent-Spin" fan; full-pressure lubrication; "Full-Flo" fuel pump*; level-mounted "Deep Breath" intake manifold; "Cushion-Quiet" engine mounting; "Equa-Flo" cooling; Waterproof Ignition System with synthetic rubber boots over tops of spark plugs; dry type air cleaner**; oil filter at extra cost.

POWER CUSHION SEMI-CENTRIFUGAL CLUTCH: dry, single plate; 9.5" outside diameter.

CONVENTIONAL TRANSMISSION: selective gear type, 3 speeds forward, one reverse; helical gears.

OVERDRIVE: optional at extra cost; fourth-speed gear that cuts in at 27 mph (approx.), cuts out at 21 mph (approx.); ratio 0.70 to 1.

FORDOMATIC DRIVE: optional at extra cost; torque converter type with 3-speed automatic planetary gear train; single stage, 3 element, hydraulic torque converter; 5-position, Semaphore Drive Selector, with illuminated quadrant, on steering column; no clutch pedal; forced air cooling.

DOUBLE-DROP FRAME: box-section side rails with specially constructed lower flanges in middle portion of frame for greater strength; 5 cross members.

INDEPENDENT FRONT WHEEL SUSPENSION: swinging link type with advanced "Hydra-Coil" springs; tubular, double-acting "Viscous Control" shock absorbers; one-piece, rubber-mounted stabilizer.

VARIABLE-RATE REAR SPRING SUSPENSION: tension type shackles; 7-leaf, semi-elliptic springs; rubber bushings at shackles and brackets and impregnated inserts between tips of upper leaves; tubular, double-acting "Viscous Control" shock absorbers.

Special fuel and vacuum pump unit, optional at extra cost, is factory-installed on all cars sold in states requiring vacuum booster windshield wiper operation and on all cars equipped with either Overdrive or Fordomatic Drive.

**Oil bath type air cleaner, optional at extra cost, is factory-installed on all cars for delivery in dust areas.*

REAR AXLE: semi-floating type; hypoid gears; ratios: with conventional drive 3.73 to 1 standard, 4.10 to 1 optional; with Overdrive 4.10 to 1 standard; with Fordomatic Drive 3.31 to 1 standard, 3.54 to 1 optional.

DOUBLE-SEAL KING-SIZE HYDRAULIC BRAKES: 4-wheel duo-servo type; composite steel and cast iron drums; molded linings; 173.1 sq. in. lining area.

CENTRAMATIC STEERING SYSTEM: Symmetrical linkage; worm and roller gear with needle-bearing mounted, triple-tooth roller; 17.7 to 1 gear ratio, 23.2 to 1 over-all steering ratio.

WHEELS AND TIRES: black sidewall 6.70 x 15 4-ply tires on 5" rims standard; white sidewalls available at extra cost.

INSTRUMENTS AND CONTROLS: "Safety-Glow" Control Panel; "Glow-Cup" control knobs with rheostat intensity regulation; "Chanalited" instrument cluster. Four-position combination starter-ignition switch; head lamp beam control switch on toe board; interior light switch on instrument panel; windshield wiper control; ventilating duct controls; T-handle controls for hood latch and parking brakes; finger-tip gearshift lever.

EQUIPMENT: (In addition to items shown or mentioned elsewhere in this folder): Extra Power dual windshield wipers; twin horns with Weatherproof mounting; rear view mirror on windshield center bar; ash tray and locking type glove compartment in instrument panel; additional ash trays in rear arm rests; interior light at each side back of quarter windows operated manually or by automatic door jamb switches; stem wound clock; cigarette lighter; Convertible type sun visors.

EXTERIOR DIMENSIONS: 114" wheelbase; 56" tread, front and rear; over-all length 197.3"; over-all width 72.9"; over-all height (loaded) 62.3"; total exposed glass area 21.0 sq. ft.

INTERIOR DIMENSIONS: hip room, front, 61.7"—rear, 48.8"; shoulder room, front, 55.4"—rear, 54.0"; head room, front, 35.7"—rear, 35.3"; leg room, front max./min., 42.8"/38.4"—leg room, rear, 37.8"; luggage compartment volume with spare tire in place, approx. 28 cu. ft.; with spare tire removed, approx. 30 cu. ft. Front seat has 4.4" fore-and-aft adjustment.

Although basically similar to the '49 and the '50 models, the 1951 Ford introduced a well-received new option, the Fordomatic Drive, an automatic transmission which did away, it was claimed, with "92% of normal driving motions" by eliminating the need to operate the clutch and the shift lever. Initially a two-speed transmission, Fordomatic started from intermediate gear (a torque converter had been added to provide controlled slippage) and shifted into high gear as the vehicle attained speed.

Coupled with the introduction of the Fordomatic was the presentation of a new key-turn starter switch which eliminated the earlier instrument panel-mounted starter button; merely by turning the ignition key to a position beyond the ON position, the starter motor was made to turn the engine, adding to the "automatic" nature of the new Ford. In the rear, a counter-balanced rear deck lid hinge balanced the lid and made it possible to reduce the size of the handle; a vacuum booster diaphram built into the fuel pump smoothed the operation of the windshield wipers. Improvements in the six-cylinder engine resulted in a Ford Six winning the Mobil Economy Run in March of 1951.

Although continuing the Crestliner (page 97) in the line in a restyled version, this model was discontinued with the introduction during the winter of the beautiful new Victoria, a two-door hard top model of far more popular appearance.

In all, Ford claimed that by looking ahead (to the motoring needs), it had **stepped ahead** with the improvements in the 1951 model.

1951 Type 73 B Custom Fordor Sedan

Mr. Robert Beck, Van Nuys, California

The side trim strip now continues across the rear.

A new hood ornament is introduced.

The 1951 front end is distinguished by its sole use of two ornamental spinners.

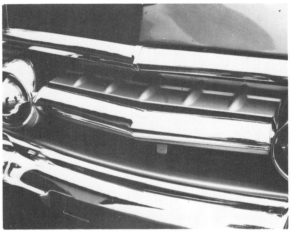

Behind the center chromed grill bar is a painted sheet metal shroud bearing stylized air baffles.

The 1951 headlight is recessed into the rim surrounding it. This head light "door" is similar to the 1950 style, but due to its greater depth, it does not interchange.

The parking light, while in the same location as last year, is now round instead of rectangular.

The grill "spinners" are pierced and formed items which no longer carry the engine designation.

New "Anti-Lock" bumper guards are designed to prevent interlocking.

116

The upholstery of the Custom Club Coupe is two-toned and bears a chromed highlight strip.

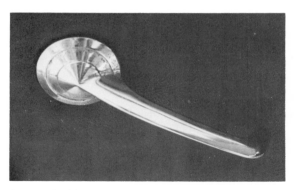

A new inside door handle eliminating the need for a separate escutcheon plate now appears.

The outside door handle is unchanged from the 1950 style.

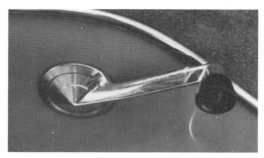

The window riser cranks, like the inside door handle, omits the escutcheon plate. A black plastic knob rotates at the outer end.

The V-8 insignia, newly styled, appears on the back of the front fender when the car is equipped with the V-8 engine.

Custom series cars have this identification plate. Deluxe series cars have an essentially similar plate bearing that series name.

A trim strip runs the length of the car and across the rear. At the front, if appropriate, the "Custom" identification plate appears. Deluxe models do not have the stripe on the side or rear.

New in 1951 is the Fordomatic transmission offered with the eight cylinder engines only. When installed, a special identification plate is placed at the rear.

The now-familiar Ford crest appears above the rear deck lid handle.

A new tail light lens design is provided (compare 1950 style on page 92).

A chromed trim cover is placed over the rear fender bulges, now called "Jet-Styled Windsplits".

118

1951 Type 72 B Custom Club Coupe Mr. William Ross, San Juan Capistrano, California

The windshield trim of the Custom line continues to be bright metal.

A new trim piece has been added to square off the appearance of the rear window.

The rear quarter window of the Custom Club Coupe pivots open; that on the Deluxe Business Coupe does not.

1951

The Crestliner, Ford's attempt to provide a sporty car with the passenger capacity of a sedan by dressing up a Tudor was continued in the line for early 1951. After the introduction of the Victoria that winter, it was, however, discontinued.

The forward portion of the airfoil design was similar to that on the 1950 model, but by incorporating the side trim of the Custom series, it became necessary to somewhat modify the rear portion (opposite page) with a resultant degradation of the appearance in the opinion of many observers.

1951 Type 70 Crestliner   Mr. William Fohrman, Suisan, California

White side wall tires are standard on the Crestliner.

The door panels of the Crestliner are upholstered in a unique pattern resembling the external air foil design.

This wheel cover is unique to the 1951 Crestliner. Resembling the one used on the 1950 model, the word FORD has been replaced with a stylized letter "F".

With the addition of the side trim stripe, the appearance of the rear quarter is greatly altered.

The V-8 insignia, referring to the only engine supplied with the Crestliner, is installed at an appropriate place on the rear fender.

Window riser handle, and inside door handle (left) are same as in other cars for this year.

Crestliner cars have chromed inside door lock knobs while other models are furnished with plastic knobs.

This pillar light is unique to the Crestliner. Two are furnished, and both are fitted with assist straps.

An outside rear view mirror on the right side is standard for the Crestliner.

The outside rear view mirror is also unique to the Crestliner, having a slender, more graceful design than others.

Radio antennas, at about this time, took on a characteristic "ring" embossed at the base of the mast. Others are found with two such rings, possibly the product of a different manufacturer.

The contrasting black side trim of the 1951 Crestliner continues to the back of the car and across the rear.

Fender shields are standard equipment on the Crestliner.

Seats are upholstered without pleats, in a plain back style highlighted by four buttons. The facing portions of the rear seat are black simulated leather.

The new name is found on an identification trim plate placed on the front fender.

The Victoria, promoted as a "top of the line" specialty car, was furnished only with the eight cylinder engine.

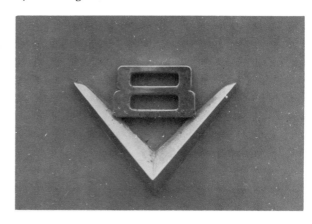

1951 Type 60 Victoria   Mr. Bill Norton, North Hollywood, California

In the late Fall of 1951, Ford introduced a new model, the Victoria, (the name had first been employed by Ford in 1931 on a Model A of no similarity whatever). A two-door car with side and rear quarter windows that rolled down completely leaving no exposed pillar, the car became known as a "two-door hard top" rather than by its given name, and the model persisted as a standard variant for the next twenty years.

Formally called the Victoria, the model was quickly accepted by the public who more frequently referred to it as a "hardtop convertible" for the appearance when the windows were lowered.

Self-edging of the side and quarter windows with bright metal mouldings enabled the designers to eliminate the "pillar" when the windows were retracted.

A new three-piece rear window on the Victoria sweeps around the corners to provide an entirely different treatment than the coupe (page 119).

The Ford crest is used decoratively on the corner "post" of the rear window.

Among the accessories on this popular Convertible Coupe are back-up lights, fuel filler door lock and dress-up trim, and full-width rear bumper guard.

1951 Type 76 Custom Convertible Coupe

Mr. Jerry Johnson, Rockford, Illinois

Folded top, retracted into a well behind the rear seat is almost completely out of sight.

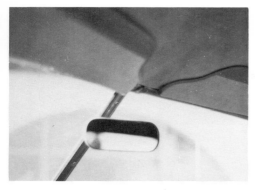

All Custom line cars had two sun visors, but the Deluxe series was provided with only one.

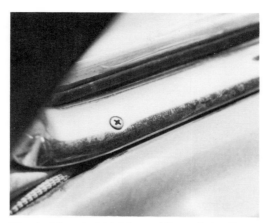

The inside windshield moulding of the Crestliner and Victoria is chrome plated; others are painted.

New design of the steering wheel results in a more unique and modern-looking rim.

At the hub of the steering wheel appears the Ford name on a background which matches that of the instrument panel itself.

MagicAire control knobs are labeled, and the separate starter push-button is eliminated, its function now incorporated into the ignition switch.

For the first time, the Magic Air Temperature System control has been recessed into the instrument panel and the unit now appears to be a *part* of the car rather than a hang-on unit.

In cases where the Magic Air extra cost option is *not* selected, a blanking plate is provided.

leather steering wheel grip is modern accessory

The entire layout of the instrument panel has been revised and no longer resembles the previous year's style. The radio speaker grill, formerly at top center, is omitted and the speaker is now placed behind the perforated panel to the right of the radio.

A glove compartment remains at the right side with push-button lock.

On either side of the optional electric clock is the cigarette lighter (left) and the ash tray. Individual cups on the instrument panel are separately lighted.

There are two radios available again this year. This is the five-tube-plus-rectifier Deluxe radio which features five push-button tuning choices, but ON/OFF is on the volume control knob.

The Custom radio is a seven-tube-plus-rectifier high fidelity set with an OFF push button and fine tuning push buttons any one of which will turn the set on. A tone control concentric with the volume control at the left of the radio, adjusts tone from MUSIC to HI FIDELITY which words appear in the window at the center of the dial.

The instruments are clustered around the speedometer in best view of the driver. At night, each is illuminated by soft light and the speed at which the car is traveling is emphasized by a ring of illumination while the rest of the scale stays dark.

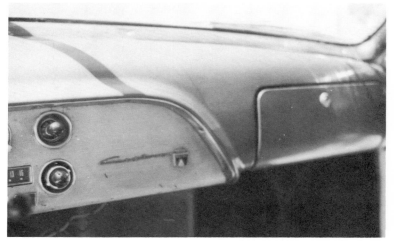

By incorporating a painted "frame" around the perforated metal instrument panel, the isolation of the controls and instruments from the passenger compartment is strongly suggested.

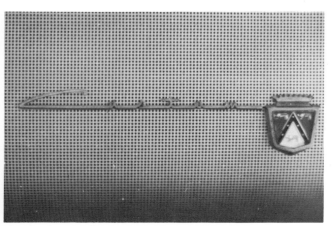

A stylized CUSTOM insignia appears with the Ford crest. Directly behind the perforated metal panel is the radio speaker.

MAINLINE AND SEDAN DELIVERY   **CUSTOMLINE**

CRESTLINE -- VICTORIA AND SUNLINER   **CRESTLINE -- COUNTRY SQUIRE**

BODY TYPES

59 A Mainline Station Wagon (Ranch Wagon)	73 A Mainline Fordor Sedan
60 B Crestline Victoria	73 B Customline Fordor Sedan
70 A Mainline Tudor Sedan	76 B Crestline Convertible Coupe (Sunliner)
70 B Customline Tudor Sedan	79 B Customline Station Wagon (Country Sedan)
72 B Customline Club Coupe	79 C Crestline Station Wagon (Country Squire)
72 C Mainline Business Coupe	

SPECIFICATIONS

SEMI-CENTRIFUGAL CLUTCH (with Conventional and Overdrive transmissions): dry, single-plate type; 9.5 in. outside diameter; new Power-Pivot pedal and linkage for softer, easier actuation; sintered bronze pilot bearing; ball type throwout bearing.

CONVENTIONAL DRIVE: selective gear type, 3 speeds forward, one reverse; all gears helical type; forged-steel synchronizers for 2nd and 3rd speeds.

OVERDRIVE (optional at extra cost): selective gear type transmission with one reverse and three forward speeds combined with a planetary gear train which provides an automatic fourth speed gear (ratio 0.70 to 1); cuts in at 27 mph (approx.) cuts out at 21 mph (approx.); manual control below instrument panel.

FORDOMATIC DRIVE (optional at extra cost): torque converter type with automatic planetary gear train; single stage, 3-element, hydraulic torque converter; hydraulic-mechanical automatic controls with no electrical or vacuum connections; forced air cooling; power transmitted through fluid member at all times. 5-position, Safety-Sequence Drive Selector on steering column.

NEW DOUBLE-DROP FRAMES: 5 cross members welded to heavy box-section side rails; new K-bar construction. Special frame construction used on Victoria, Sunliner, Ranch Wagon and Country Squire.

INDEPENDENT FRONT WHEEL SUSPENSION: swinging link type with tailored-to-model Hydra-Coil springs; new, tubular double-acting Viscous Control shock absorbers; new, one-piece, rubber-mounted stabilizer.

NEW VARIABLE-RATE REAR SPRING SUSPENSION: new longer 7-leaf, semi-elliptic springs, longitudinally mounted; rubber bushings at shackles and brackets; impregnated inserts between tips of upper leaves; tension type shackles; new tubular, double-acting, diagonally-mounted, Viscous Control shock absorbers. Ranch Wagon and Country Squire have 9-leaf semi-elliptic springs.

REAR AXLE: semi-floating type; hypoid gears; forged axle shafts with integral flanges; welded pressed-steel banjo-type housing with rear cover welded in place. Higher capacity axle used in Ranch Wagon and Country Squire has composite type housing. Ratios, V-8 or SIX engine and Conventional Drive; all Sedans and Coupes, 3.90 to 1 std., 4.10 to 1 optional; Ranch Wagon and Country Squire, 4.09 to 1 std., 4.27 to 1 optional. Ratios, V-8 or SIX engine and Overdrive: all Sedans and Coupes, 4.10 to 1 std., 3.90, 3.31, or 3.15 to 1 optional; Ranch Wagon and Country Squire, 4.27 to 1 std. Ratios, V-8 or SIX engine and Fordomatic: all Sedans and Coupes, 3.31 to 1 standard, 3.54 to 1 optional; Ranch Wagon and Country Squire 3.54 to 1 standard.

DOUBLE-SEAL HYDRAULIC BRAKES: new Power-Pivot pedal actuation of 4-wheel duo-servo type brakes; more effectively double-sealed rear brakes; 11" diameter composite steel and cast iron drums on Ranch Wagon and Country Squire; 10" on other models; molded linings. 159.1 sq. in. lining area on Ranch Wagon and Country Squire, 173.5 sq. in. other models. Easier-action hand brake.

NEW, EASIER STEERING: new symmetrical linkage with spring-loaded ball-stud in steering cross link; new 90°-mounted worm and roller type gear with triple-tooth roller on needle-bearing; 18.2 to 1 gear ratio; 26.3 to 1 over-all steering ratio; 18 in. diameter steering wheel.

WHEELS AND TIRES: 6.00 x 16 4-ply tires on 4½" rims standard, with 6.70 x 15 4-ply tires on 5" rims optional at extra cost on Mainline Sedans and Coupes; 6.70 x 15 4-ply tires on 5" rims standard on Customline models, and on Sunliner and Victoria with Conventional or Overdrive transmission; 7.10 x 15 4-ply tires on 5" rims on Sunliner and Victoria equipped with Fordomatic; 7.10 x 15 6-ply tires standard on Ranch Wagon and Country Squire.

EXTERIOR DIMENSIONS: 115" wheelbase; 58" front and 56" rear treads; over-all width, 73.9" (Country Squire 74.3"); over-all length, 197.8".

EXTERIOR COLOR AND UPHOLSTERY COMBINATIONS: See chart showing exterior color—interior trim combinations in front portion of this catalog.

INSTRUMENTS AND CONTROLS: new Flight-Style Control Panel with illuminated bezels around 4-position combination starter-ignition switch and around control knobs for windshield wipers, main light switch, controls for ventilating air ducts, interior light switch, cigarette lighter (except Mainline) and choke control. New, indirectly illuminated instrument cluster has oil pressure, fuel level, water temperature and battery charge indicators grouped around the semicircle speedometer dial with odometer located at center. T-handle for parking brake on lower left edge of panel; head lamp beam control switch on toe board; fingertip gearshift lever on steering column; new hood latch and safety catch operated from front by separate levers.

EQUIPMENT STANDARD ON ALL MODELS: new Flight-Style Control Panel with ash tray and locking type parcel compartment; new dual windshield wipers; twin horns with weatherproof mounting; rear view mirror on windshield upper molding; integral foot rest in rear compartment; new two-spoke, black plastic steering wheel; interior light operated by manual switch on instrument panel.

New contour-type seats with pillow backs; new Automatic Posture Control front seat mechanism; improved non-sag front seat construction with heavier foam-rubber pad in cushion; new non-sag rear seat construction with foam rubber pad in cushion.

New bright metal belt molding; nameplate on front fenders or doors; V-8 insignia on front fenders and on instrument panels of V-8 models; Fordomatic or Overdrive nameplate on deck lid or tailgate of cars so equipped; rain shields at front vent windows; modernistic dual tail lamps.

MAINLINE STANDARD EQUIPMENT: sun visor on driver's side; horn button at center of steering wheel; ribbed-rubber shield over lower part of body side embossments; black rubber mats, front and rear (except Ranch Wagon load space); black rubber exterior reveal molding at windshield and rear window; coat hooks (except Ranch Wagon).

Ranch Wagon has "Stowaway" rear seat; counterbalanced-type lift gate hinges; two support arms on tailgate with manual release; rotary type lift gate and tailgate latches; one-piece curved window in lift gate; ribbed tan linoleum floor covering in load space; gas filler cap at left rear of body.

CUSTOMLINE STANDARD EQUIPMENT: two sun visors; full-circle horn ring with special button at center; bright metal exterior reveal molding at windshield and rear window; two interior lights operated by automatic door switches in addition to manual control; bright metal molding on body sides; arm rests, front and rear; one ash tray in rear compartment of Fordor, two in others; robe cord in Fordor, assist loops in others. Customline nameplate and bright metal molding on instrument panel; cigarette lighter; stem-wound clock; pebble-grain rubber mat in rear in colors to harmonize with interior trim; bright metal cap moldings on side embossments.

CRESTLINE STANDARD EQUIPMENT: (in addition to or in place of Customline items). Sunliner: two robe cords; arm rests in front only; Sunliner name on door molding; interior light under instrument panel, operated manually and automatically by door switches.

Victoria: two robe cords; built-in type arm rests in rear with ash trays incorporated; carpets, front and rear, in shades harmonizing with interior trim; special, bright-metal rear window exterior molding; gold-finished crest, each side, back of quarter windows; Victoria name on door molding.

Country Squire: "Stowaway" center seat; two-piece removable rear seat; arm rests on front doors only; no coat hooks; wood molding on side embossments; counterbalanced type lift gate hinges; two support arms, with manual release, on tailgate; one-piece curved window in lift gate; ribbed tan linoleum floor covering in load space; gas filler cap at left rear of body.

1952 saw an increase in wheelbase to 115" with accompanying increases in width and length to provide a larger car. Changes in the appearance of the car were made, and thinner windshield corner posts and one piece curved windshields (and rear windows) joined to give the appearance of a "bigger" car.

Ford introduced a **third** line in 1952 and redesigned the earlier two. The Crestline (formerly the Custom), the Customline (formerly the DeLuxe) joined the new Mainline which was the lowest price, or economy version. A new overhead valve six cylinder engine was available optionally in all but the Crestline models.

Modifications made to bodies included the relocation of the fuel filler to a position behind the license plate at the center rear (to allow filling from either side), and an exceptionally accessible hood latch located at the front. The new 101 HP high compression SIX now had enough power to function correctly with the Fordomatic, which, like Overdrive was offered as an optional accessory in place of the conventional three-speed manual transmission, and the brake pedal (and clutch, when used) were suspended from above "cleaning up" the floorboard area.

Ford's list of available optional accessories had now reached over 30, not including cleaners, waxes, polishes, and lubricating and maintenance items. Truly Ford had become a "Big car".

1952 Type 60 Victoria

The Victoria had caught the public's eye and it was truly a dressed-up Ford. With the windows up it was snug as a sedan; down, it offered almost as much excitement as a Convertible. Ford called it "beauty that belongs".

Mr. Howard Lampke, Orange, California

The hood opens from the front, is hinged at the rear. A hood release latch is located at the front, and no inside cable is used to unlock the hood.

The See Clear windshield wiper accessory functions by directing two streams of water from a rubber bag under the hood through this dual-nozzle.

The wide rear window of the Victoria is composed of three pieces installed to provide a maximum wrap-around unit with considerably more rear vision than the standard unit.

The Ford crest is used again in 1952 at the front of the hood.

A new hood ornament, now all-metal, replaces the earlier styles which incorporated plastic fins.

Headlights are recessed further, and the headlamp "door" is now designed to appear as an extension of the fender itself and painted to match. A chromed inner ring retains a suggestion of the abandoned chrome doors.

A type of "spinner" remains on the grill, but unlike the dual arrangement of 1951, only a single unit is used, once again directly in the center.

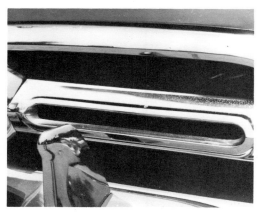

Formed, pierced, and chromed horizontal grill bars are styled to suggest added intake air capacity.

Parking lights are placed at the ends of the radiator grill and appear more elaborate than previously.

The wide one-piece windshield is framed in bright metal. The chromed part on the hood is the jet spray nozzle of the optional "see-clear" windshield-washer accessory.

The vent wing assembly, including the major section just forward of the glass is made of stainless steel. Curiously, *this* part was replaced in the 1953 series with an interchangeable chromed casting which weathered badly.

15" wheels are standard on the Customline and Crestline series and optional on the Mainlines which still have standard 16" wheels. The white sidewall tires and dress-up wheel cover are optional extras.

The side trim commences with a piece reminiscent of that on the 1950 series (page 107) but does not now bear the series designation.

If appropriate, the V-8, indicating the engine choice appears, with the series name on the front fenders. The trim strip beneath them is applied to the Customline and Crestline series only and is omitted on the low-priced Mainline series.

The side trim stripe ends on the door and is followed by a dress-up simulated scoop on the rear fender.

With the windows retracted, the Victoria offers an unobstructed view.

The name is now stamped into the window sill trim.

Similar to the preceeding model (page 125), the design of the rear roof quarter *has* been changed. In addition to minor geometrical changes, the Ford crest now appears within an embossed circle.

The simulated rear fender "scoop" suggests a rear-engine installation.

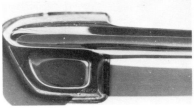

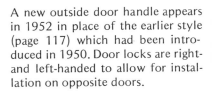
A new outside door handle appears in 1952 in place of the earlier style (page 117) which had been introduced in 1950. Door locks are right- and left-handed to allow for installation on opposite doors.

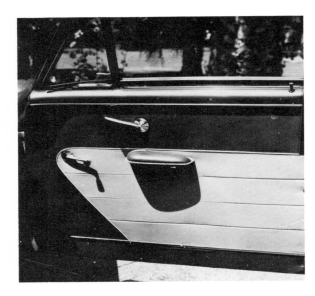

Upholstery design of the 1952 Victoria door in some ways resembles the earlier Crestliner design (page 121).

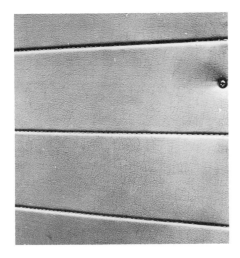

A long-wearing, simulated leather, panel is used on the doors, harmonizing with the upholstery choice.

Inside door handles and window risers are unchanged from 1951.

Plastic inside door lock knobs protrude through the door panel.

New in 1952 is the combination data and patent plate which for this year exclusively was placed on the right hand door pillar. Just above the data plate is one of two switches placed in the front doors of the Crestline and Customline to operate the interior lights, a system first introduced on the 1950 Custom Deluxe models.

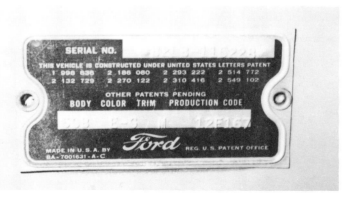

In addition to stating the extensive patent covering, the new data plates also establish, in addition to the serial number, certain other items, including body, exterior paint, interior trim, and the date of manufacture of the car.

A new round pillar light with a translucent plastic cover is introduced in 1952. Moulded into the cover is the Ford crest. The simple formed garment hangers are also new this year. The handle in the lower right corner operates the rear quarter window.

A set of Ford fiber seat covers has been installed over the original interior. The Victoria was available in a choice of 6 single-tone and six two-tone interiors, the largest selection of any car in the Ford line in 1952.

The three piece three-pointed-star set is standard trim in the Victoria, but the motif is carried out in accessory trim available for *all* cars.

The three piece construction of the Victoria rear window is continued in 1952.

Counterbalanced hinges had been placed on the deck lid in 1951 greatly easing the opening. In 1952, the Ford Crest was fitted into a chromed frame and became the deck lid handle. Beneath it is the keylock. Simply by turning the key and releasing the latch, the lid would swing up.

Ford introduced "center fill" fuel tank filler tubes this year. By swinging the license plate down and out of the way, the filler tube and cap were exposed.

A star-shaped plastic trim ring, chromed in appearance, is placed over the red glass lens as a dress-up item. The chromed outer ring is part of the tail light housing assembly.

Tail lights are styled as an extension of the vestigal rear fenders. Inside are two-filament bulbs for stop or parking illumination. Turn signals continue to be an option, but if selected, operate the appropriate stop light.

A new chromed Fordomatic identification plate appears this year on cars so equipped.

Another instrument panel overhaul brings the "Flight-Style Control Panel" with the beginnings of a shroud over the instrument cluster and the elimination of the perforated metal used in 1951.

A full-circle horn ring is furnished on the Crestline and Customline cars. Mainline cars are not equipped with the horn ring, but all share the two-spoke black plastic steering wheel.

A restyled hub button on the steering column finds the Ford crest again in evidence as well as a styled Ford name. The Mainline hub is plain.

Again resembling a hang-on unit, the control head for the optional Magic Air system is installed below the instrument panel. The fan motor control is, however, placed in the cluster of four knobs just above it (upper right photo).

The four control knobs are for the interior lights, the cigarette lighter (omitted in Mainline), and the choke, all standard, plus, (lower left) the blower switch for the optional Magic Air System. If the optional accessory system is not installed, a knob in this position would operate the right air duct, a function otherwise included in the accessory.

Balancing the four control knobs to the right of the steering column are these four on the left which include windshield wiper, lights, left air, and the four-position combination ignition lock and starter switch introduced in 1951. Knobs are restyled (page 127) and are slightly concave.

A locking glove compartment, standard on all models remains at the right side of the instrument panel. Above it are placed, as appropriate, the V-8 indicating that engine, and either Crestline or Customline script; Mainline series lacks such dress-up items.

Gauges for Oil Pressure, Water temperature, Battery charge, and fuel level are grouped around a semi-circular speedometer. The instrument panel is shaped to form a shroud over the assembly.

An optional electric clock is placed at the top center of the instrument panel. When not purchased, blanking plate covers the mounting hole.

Again in 1952, there are two radio choices. This is the Ford Deluxe radio with five tubes (plus rectifier) and five-station push button tuning. Also available is the "big" radio, the Ford Custom seven tube (plus rectifier) set which has the five push buttons and four-position tone control (see page 128).

If a radio is installed, its speaker is placed behind this perforated-metal grill section in the instrument panel.

MAINLINE AND SEDAN DELIVERY   **CUSTOMLINE**

CRESTLINE -- VICTORIA AND SUNLINER   **CRESTLINE -- COUNTRY SQUIRE**

BODY TYPES

59 A Mainline Station Wagon (Ranch Wagon)	73 A Mainline Fordor Sedan
60 B Crestline Victoria	73 B Customline Fordor Sedan
70 A Mainline Tudor Sedan	76 B Crestline Convertible Coupe (Sunliner)
70 B Customline Tudor Sedan	78 A Sedan Delivery (Courier)
72 B Customline Club Coupe	79 B Customline Station Wagon (Country Sedan)
72 C Mainline Business Coupe	79 C Crestline Station Wagon (Country Squire)

SPECIFICATIONS

SPECIFICATIONS

Choice of Two Great Engines

Strato-Star V-8: 110 brake horsepower @ 3800 rpm; 32.5 taxable h.p.; 7.2 to 1 compression ratio; 3.19 in. bore x 3.75 in. stroke; 239.4 cu. in. displacement; L-head type; dual downdraft carburetor with dry-type air cleaner;* Full-Flo fuel pump;** by-pass type oil filter (at extra cost). 15-plate, 90 amp-hr. battery.

Mileage Maker Six: 101 brake horsepower @ 3500 rpm; 30.4 taxable h.p.; 7.0 to 1 compression ratio; 3.56 in. bore x 3.6 in. stroke; 215.3 cu. in. displacement; overhead valves; unit-design downdraft carburetor with dry-type air cleaner;* Full-Flo fuel pump;** full-flow oil filter (at extra cost). 15-plate, 90 amp-hr. battery.

Both V-8 and Six have these "worth more" features: Automatic Power Pilot, Ford's exclusive carburetion-ignition-combustion system; free-turning valves, exclusive to Ford in its field; precision-molded, superior alloy crankshaft, a Ford exclusive in the industry; high-alloy cast steel exhaust valves, another Ford exclusive; super-fitted aluminum alloy pistons, the finest type in the industry; waterproof ignition for quick, sure starts in all kinds of weather; key-turn starting for extra convenience.

Beautiful Baked Enamel
Body Colors

Single-Tone: Raven Black, Woodsmoke Gray, Sheridan Blue, Glacier Blue, Timberline Green, Fern Mist Green, Seafoam Green, Polynesian Bronze, Sandpiper Tan, Carnival Red.

Two-Tone (at extra cost): Carnival Red with Sungate Ivory top; Glacier Blue with Sheridan Blue top; Seafoam Green with Timberline Green top.

Modern Interiors

5 Color-Harmonized Interiors: Two-tone Gray Stripe Craftcord, Green and White Diagonal Stripe Craftweave or Two-tone Tan Check Craftweave upholstery to harmonize with exterior colors; seat bolsters and headlining in harmonizing darker shades; 2-tone vinyl-and-cloth door and quarter panel trim. Painted surfaces are in rich gray, green or brown metallic. Pebbled rubber floor mats—black in front, colored in rear. Blue and Ivory or Mahogany and Ivory Saddletex (vinyl) upholstery and trim at extra cost.

Fittings and Controls: 2 sun visors; arm rests front and rear; parking brake handle at left of steering wheel; 2 pillar l___ operated by door switches or knob on instrument panel; lighting of instruments and controls regulated by turning headlight knob; ash tray in front, 2 in rear; 4-position starter-ignition switch; cigarette lighter; stem-wound clock; coat hooks; 2 assist loops.

Choice of Three Great Drives

Fordomatic Drive (at extra cost)—fluid torque converter combined with automatic planetary gear train; Safety Sequence Drive Selector on steering column; no clutch pedal. **Overdrive** (at extra cost)—conventional 3-speed selective gear type transmission plus planetary gear unit which provides 4th speed ratio (0.70 to 1) automatically. **Conventional Drive—** 3-speed selective gear type; helical gears; synchronizers for 2nd and 3rd speeds.

Rugged Chassis

Rear Axle: hypoid gear type. Ratio (to 1): with Conventional—3.90 std., 4.10 opt.; with Overdrive—4.10 std., 3.90 or 3.31 opt.; with Fordomatic—3.31 std., 3.54 opt.

Magic Action Brakes: duo-servo type; 10 in. dia. drums; molded linings, total area 173.5 sq. in. Double seal between drum and backing plate. Power-Pivot pedal mounting; master cylinder on front of dash, under hood.

Balanced-Ease Steering: Symmetrical linkage with spring loaded ball in cross link. Worm and triple-tooth sector gear.

Tires and Wheels: 6.70 x 15 4-ply on 5 in. rims. Black side walls standard; white sidewalls optional at extra cost.

Semi-Centrifugal Clutch: (with Conventional and Overdrive transmissions): dry, single plate type; 9.5 in. outside diameter; ball-type throwout bearing; Power-Pivot pedal mounting.

Independent Front Wheel Suspension: tailored-to-weight Hydra-Coil springs with Viscous Control shock absorbers; one-piece torsional stabilizer bar.

Variable Rate Rear Suspension: semi-elliptic Para-Flex springs; rubber-bushed brackets and tension-type shackles; diagonally mounted Viscous Control shock absorbers.

Frame: box-section side rails; 5 cross members; center cross member and diagonal struts form rigid K-bar.

Exterior Dimensions

115 in. wheelbase; 58 in. front, 56 in. rear tread; 197.8 in. long; 74.3 in. wide; 61.9 in. high (with normal load).

*Oil bath type air cleaner, optional at extra cost, is factory installed on all cars for delivery in dust areas.

**Special fuel and vacuum pump unit, optional at extra cost, is factory installed on all cars sold in states requiring vacuum booster windshield wiper operation and on all cars equipped with Overdrive or Fordomatic Drive.

1953 saw the release of a modestly restyled Ford. Instrument panel, front end, rear deck, and side trim were all redone, but there was no basic and substantial change comparable to the introduction of the long-lived Fordomatic in 1951 or the completely new front suspension in 1949. However, a 1953 Crestline Sunliner (convertible) was chosen as pace car for the Indianapolis 500.

At the rear, tail lights were restyled and a decorative handle was returned to the deck lid; side trim was altered (a decorative stripe was added to the Crestliner rear fender), and in front a simplification of the center "hub" reduced costs in its manufacture.

Engines were unchanged from 1952, but despite the limited changes in the model year, Ford's advertising people were still able to come up with some 41 items justifying the "worth more" features of the car. It appeared that the ultimate had been reached and that the Ford **was** the "Standard of the American Road", a classic example of a **double entendre.** Was the Ford the Standard (flag or banner) of "The American Road" (Ford's mailing address), or was it the Standard (established measure) of the American Road (the nation's highways)?

Type 60 B Crestline Victoria

Mr. Tom Howard, Buena Park, California

A two-diaphram fuel pump became available in 1953 and was furnished by Ford on all cars sold in those states requiring a booster on the vacuum windshield wipers, and also on all cars equipped with accessory transmissions.

A newly styled hood ornament reflected the contemporary interest in rocket technology.

The Ford Crest appears on the hood at the front center.

Headlights are now further recessed and the "door" a more integral looking part of the fender.

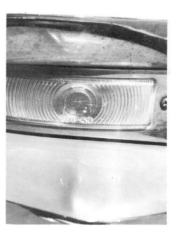

Rectangular parking lights recessed into a protected position behind the bumpers also serve as turn signal lights when that extra-cost option is selected.

The hood is hinged at the rear and opens from the front.

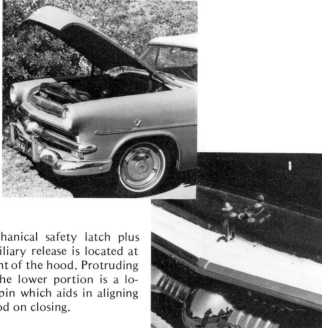

A mechanical safety latch plus an auxiliary release is located at the front of the hood. Protruding from the lower portion is a locating pin which aids in aligning the hood on closing.

A long side trim strip extends down the side of the Crestline and the Customline series.

An additional trim strip appears on the rear fenders of the Crestline and Customline but is omitted on the Mainline series. The rear fender shields are accessories.

This simulated rear fender "scoop" is in keeping with the suggestion of a rear-engined car, a consideration that was receiving popular interest at the time although Ford did not appear to seriously entertain such thoughts. The Mainline series has a smaller, less attractive trim.

f the V-8 engine appeared in the car, it was decorated with this insignia on the front fenders. Initially (1951) manufactured of rustless (stainless) steel, chrome plated units were introduced during 1952 and used hrough 1953.

At the front of the side trim strip appears a chromed identification plate stating the series name. (The Customline series plate was essentially the same.) Mainline, since it did not have the balance of the long trim strip had a slightly different, but substantially identical plate.

The rear quarter windows pivot out of sight.

A significant feature of the Victoria is the fact that with the windows retracted there is the complete absence of the window pillar and passengers can obtain a completely unobstructed view.

The 1953 Victoria resembles the 1952 model in this area.

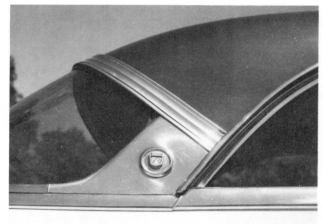

Two crimped rings encircle the base of this 1953 passenger car antenna. Previously, (compare page 123) and later, there appeared similar antennae with only one such ring.

The Victoria name is placed on the window sill.

The outside door handle is unchanged from 1952. The inside door lock knob is again formed from plastic.

Victoria, and Skyliner, windows are framed in rustless steel.

The same chromed inside door handles are used again in 1953 as first introduced in 1951.

An improved, push-button released, rotary door lock appears on the 1953 Ford.

This data plate appears on the left hand door pillar just below the switch which automatically lights the interior lights when the door is opened.

The back-up lights are an accessory on this 1953 Victoria.

The rear deck lid handle returns this year as a housing for the key lock which is placed at its center. Above the handle is the familiar Ford crest.

Jacking instructions are placed on the inside of the lid, near the right hinge where they may easily be read.

Spring-loaded counter-balanced rear deck lid hinges, introduced on the 1952 model make opening of the deck lid far easier.

A wide luggage storage compartment is provided. The spare tire now mounts in a partial well at the right side of the compartment.

The tail light lens of 1953 is fitted with a plastic bright metal-like sleeve over the inner portion unlike the 1952 lens which had a more elaborate star-shaped trim, (page 142) but the outer ring, part of the light housing itself, is identical.

These bumper guards, first used in 1952, are unchanged.

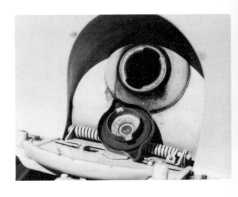

A black plastic knob is used on the gearshift lever.

The steering wheel on the Main-line has no horn ring, but those on the Crestline and Customline are fitted with this half-circle.

1953 marks the 50th anniversary of the Ford Motor Company, and the horn button is suitably inscribed for the occasion.

The electric clock is mounted at the top center of the instrument panel.

The instrument gauges have been removed from the speedometer itself and are now clustered around it under a protective shroud formed by the instrument panel.

The Fordomatic position indicator is placed semaphore-style on the steering column.

Located to the right of the steering column are control knobs for interior lights, cigarette lighter, choke, and the blower for the Magic Air Temperature System.

The radio speaker is concealed behind the perforated metal grill placed in the instrument panel.

An ashtray is located in the instrument panel just below the push-button radio.

Suspended just below the instrument panel is the control unit for the Magic Air Temperature System.

A locking glove compartment at the right side of the instrument panel is standard. Above it appears the V-8 emblem when that engine is chosen.

1953 Type 73 B Customline Fordor Sedan

Mr. Tom Howard, Buena Park, California

In similar fashion to the Crestline (page 151), the Customline name is placed in an insignia trim plate on the front fenders. The V-8 again signifies engine choice.

The Sedans have a relatively wide fixed pillar between the front and rear windows, and lack the more elaborate chrome trim of the windshield post as found on Victorias and Convertibles.

A vent window is standard in the rear windows of the Fordor sedans, although the one in the Mainline Fordor sedan does not open.

The Customline, like the Crestline, has two pillar lights which are operated either by the switches in the front doors, or turning the headlight switch knob. In the Mainline, only one pillar light, on the left side, is furnished and it has a separate switch on the instrument panel.

This is one of the original interior choices for the Customline Fordor sedan, gray striped "Craftcord", a mohair-like fabric.

If applicable, either Fordomatic or Overdrive script plates are attached to the deck lid.

The Sunliner name is embossed in the window sill.

A stainless steel trough serves to deflect rain water from entering the vent windows which may be open for ventilation.

1953 Type 76 B Crestline Convertible Coupe (Sunliner)

Mr. John Simms   Spring Valley, California

A single wide door opens to admit passengers to either the front or rear seat.

With windows retracted, no pillar remains to obscure view or intrude on access.

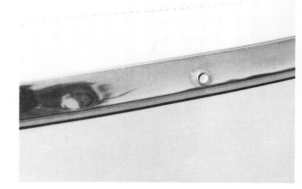

A series of snaps are provided to which a cover may be fastened when the folded top is lowered into the well behind the rear seat.

1946 Type 79 B Super De Luxe Station Wagon

1946 Type 76 Super De Luxe Convertible Club Coupe

1947 Type 76 Super De Luxe Convertible Club Coupe

1947 Type 71 Sportsman

1947 Type 70-B Super De Luxe Tudor sedan

1949 Type 72 B Ford Custom Club Coupe

1949 Type 79 Ford Custom Station Wagon

1950 Type 76B Custom Deluxe Convertible Coupe

(See page 107 for trim accessories.)

1950 Type 70B Custom Deluxe Tudor sedan

1950 Type 70C Crestliner

1951 Type 70 Crestliner

1951 Type 60 Victoria

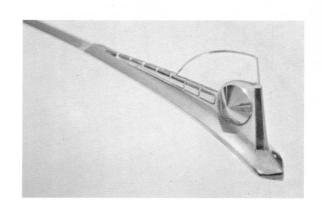

1950 Type 72B Deluxe Club Coupe

(Note accessory Sun Visor.)

1952 Type 60 Victoria

1953 Type 73B Customline Fordor Sedan

1953 Type 76B Crestline Convertible Coupe (Sunliner)

1953 Type 60B Crestline Victoria

1954 Type 60F Skyliner

1955 Type 73C Fairlane TownSedan

1955 Type 79 B Country Sedan

1955 Type 60B Fairlane Victoria

The mid-Fifties saw the use of two-tone paint schemes that resulted in a never-since duplicated array of color. From the left is a two-tone 1954, a 1955, and a 1956 model providing a fascinating example of what it was like then. By the end of the decade, solid colors were again the vogue, and the end of brightness was imminent.

1956 Type 76B Fairlane Convertible Coupe

1956 Type 70C Fairlane Club Sedan

1956 Type 64A Fairlane Crown Victoria

1957 Type 64B Fairlane Club Sedan

1957 Type 63A Fairlane 500 Club Victoria

1957 Type 76B Fairlane 500 Convertible Coupe

1958 Type 59A Ranch Wagon

1957 Type 51A Fairlane 500 Skyliner

1959 Type 51A Galaxie Hide-Away Hardtop (Skyliner)

Although the name SKYLINER had first appeared in 1954 on the plastic-roofed victoria and was then discarded, it was reassigned, starting in 1957, to an ingenious new variation on which the entire metal roof could be automatically retracted into the trunk. Despite its attractive appearance, this true "hard top" Convertible model persisted only through 1959 and was then dropped.

A 1954 Victoria is flanked by a pair of 1954 Skyliners

"More Than Ever, the Standard of the American Road"

Ford rebounded with a whole list of improvements and innovations in the 1954 models. Foremost was the exciting list of Power Options that included power-lift windows, master-glide power steering, swift-sure power brakes, and 4-way power seats. Instrument panels were again redesigned and the radio speaker placed at the top center of the dashboard from which it had been moved in 1949. "Idiot lights" replaced the oil pressure and radiator coolant temperature instruments of the past, and New Ball Joint Front Suspension was introduced.

The big news though was the introduction of a new V-8 engine, with overhead valves, (catching up with the 1952 introduction of the OHV Ford SIX) now rated at 130 hp, almost 25% more than the 1953 flathead. Although it has grown, been enlarged, redesigned, and evolved, the 1954 OHV Ford V-8 engine marks the start of engine production that is basically unchanged through the next twenty years.

Addtionally, Ford's innovative Designers produced the exciting new "Skyliner", a modified Victoria in which a tinted plastic insert was placed in the roof to combine the protection of a closed car with the exhileration of a Convertible. The concept was further extended in an optional accessory green-tinted transparent plastic insert which ran from the front header to the first bow of the Convertible top.

Another of Ford's new ideas was the Automatic Rain Guard first offered this year (and of which there is no record of one having been **produced**) in which a sensor, (according to Popular Mechanics Magazine), was placed on the rear seat to activate the automatic top mechanism in the event of unexpected rain showers. No intra-connection was offered though with the power-lift windows.

In all, 1954 saw Ford offer everything that appeared in the 1953 "Standard of the American Road" and they had **added** the new V-8 engine and some other innovations. Correctly, their catalogs described the 1954 model as "more than ever The Standard of the American Road".

Type 76 B Crestline Convertible Coupe

Photographed in early 1954 in Victoria, B. C. Canada, by Glenn Embree, this popular Sunliner had already been made roadworthy. Accessory curb guards protect the whitewall tires from scuffing!

MAINLINE

CUSTOMLINE

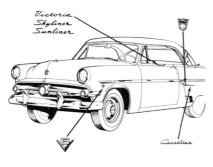

CRESTLINE -- VICTORIA, SKYLINER AND SUNLINER

CRESTLINE -- COUNTRY SQUIRE

BODY TYPES

59 A Mainline Ranch Wagon	59 B Customline Ranch Wagon	60 B Crestline Victoria
70 A Mainline Tudor Sedan	70 B Customline Tudor Sedan	60 F Crestline Skyliner
72 C Mainline Business Coupe	72 B Customline Club Coupe	73 C Crestline Fordor Sedan
73 A Mainline Fordor Sedan	73 B Customline Fordor Sedan	76 B Crestline Convertible Coupe (Sunliner)
	79 B Customline Country Sedan	79 C Crestline Country Squire

SPECIFICATIONS

Y-Block V-8 Engine: 130-h.p. @ 4200 r.p.m.; 39.2 taxable h.p.; 239 cu. in. displacement; 3.50 in. bore x 3.10 in. stroke; 7.2 to 1 compression ratio.

I-Block Mileage Maker Six Engine: 115 h.p. @ 3900 r.p.m.; 31.5 taxable h.p.; 223 cu. in. displacement; 3.62 in. bore x 3.60 in. stroke; 7.2 to 1 compression ratio.

Semi-Centrifugal Clutch (with Conventional and Overdrive transmissions): dry, single-plate type; 9.5 in. dia. with Six, 10 in. dia. with V-8; sintered bronze pilot bearing; ball-type throwout bearing.

Conventional Drive: 3 speeds forward, one reverse; all gears helical type.

Overdrive (optional at extra cost): 3-speed transmission, planetary gear train provides automatic 4th gear; cuts in at 27 mph (approx.), cuts out at 21 mph (approx.).

Fordomatic Drive (optional at extra cost): single stage, 3-element, hydraulic torque converter; with automatic planetary gear train; forced air cooling.

New Double-Drop Frames: 5 cross-member type; stronger box-section side rails; K-bar construction; Special designs for Victoria, Skyliner, Sunliner and station wagons.

New Ball-Joint Front Wheel Suspension: rubber-bushed; transverse-link type with ball-joints; tailored-to-weight coil springs; new full-displacement tubular shock absorbers.

New Variable-Rate Rear Spring Suspension: new 5-leaf semi-elliptic springs, rubber-bushed brackets and tension-type shackles; inserts between all leaves; new diagonally-mounted tubular shock absorbers. Station Wagons have 9-leaf design.

Rear Axle: semi-floating type; hypoid gears; welded steel, banjo-type housing. Axle in station wagon models has composite housing.

New Hydraulic Brakes: more rugged duo-servo brakes, Double-Seal type; 11″ dia. drums on station wagon models, 10″ dia. on other models; 159.1 sq. in. lining area, station wagon models, 173.5 sq. in., other models.

Wheels and Tires: Mainline and Customline Sedans and Coupes, Crestline Fordor—6.70 x 15 4-ply tires std.; Sunliner, Victoria and Skyliner with Conventional or Overdrive—6.70 x 15 4-ply tires std.—with Fordomatic 7.10 x 15 4-ply tires std.; Ranch Wagons—7.10 x 15 4-ply tires std., 6-ply optional at extra cost; Country Sedan and Country Squire—7.10 x 15 6-ply tires std.

Exterior Dimensions: 115.5″ wheelbase; width, Mainline models, Customline Ranch Wagon 73.2″, all others 73.5″; length, station wagons 198.1″, all others 198.3″; height (design load), Mainline and Customline Sedans 62.3″, Club and Business Coupes 61.9″, Sunliner 61.1″, Victoria and Skyliner 60.7″, station wagons 63.9″.

New, Easier Steering: 25.3 to 1 over-all steering ratio; 18″ dia. steering wheel.

Equipment Standard on All Models: Astra-Dial Control Panel; dual windshield wipers; interior light with manual switch; front seat Automatic Posture Control; non-sag seat construction; cotton padding in seat backs.

Mainline Standard Equipment: sun visor; horn button; single horn; rubber floor mats; coat hooks; cotton-padded seat cushions. Ranch Wagon has Stowaway rear seat; counterbalanced lift gate; support arms, with manual release on tail gate.

Customline Standard Equipment: two sun visors; half-circle horn ring; twin horns; dome light, integral switch, automatic door switches; arm rests, front and rear; ash tray in Fordor rear compartment, two in others; assist straps, Tudor, Club Coupe; cigarette lighter; stem-wind clock; rubber floor mats; foam rubber in seat cushions. Country Sedan has interior features listed below for Country Squire.

Crestline Standard Equipment: (in addition to or in place of Customline items).

Sunliner: two robe cords; arm rests front only; light and switch under panel, also operated by door switches; top control at lower left of control panel.

Victoria and Skyliner: two robe cords; arm rests in rear with ash trays; carpets, front and rear (except Victoria with all-vinyl trim); bright metal drip molding; gold finished crests at sides of back window; interior light each side of back window operated manually and automatically. Skyliner has 2-piece, traverse-type, fabric sun shield.

Fordor: robe cord and ash tray in rear; colored steering wheel and column; 2-tone control panel; carpets, front and rear; bright-metal molding across tops of doors; bright-metal trim at sides of back window; bright-metal drip molding.

Country Squire: Stowaway center seat; two-piece removable rear seat; arm rests on front and rear doors; counterbalanced type lift gate hinges; two support arms, with manual release, on tail gate; maple-grained glass fiber moldings on body sides and tail gate; colored ribbed linoleum in load space.

NOTE: *Special fuel and vacuum pump unit, optional at extra cost, is factory-installed on all cars sold in states requiring vacuum booster windshield wiper operation and on all cars equipped with Overdrive or Fordomatic Drive. Oil bath type air cleaner, optional at extra cost, is factory installed on all cars for delivery in dust areas.*

Ford had an unusual idea in 1954 when they modified the Victoria to produce a new model, the Skyliner which had a tinted plastic insert in the roof over the front seat (a parallel offering was a modification to the Convertible top incorporating a similar, light weight tinted vinyl from front header to the first bow).

Even with windows closed, the Skyliner presents an "open air" feeling that cannot be duplicated. Overhead vision is excellent, a boon to sight-seeing, and for privacy, or in the case of extreme heat, a snap-in liner provides the protection required.

With special upholstery stylings, the Skyliner is easily one of the most unusual and rare cars that Ford ever built.

1954

In 1954, in addition to a new engine, Ford went to a Ball Joint front suspension replacing the king pins that had been typical of Ford for thirty years.

Bumpers wrap firmly around the front fenders, and parking lights are contained in the ends of the center grill bar.

Commencing with the 1953 model, the center grill bar also curves around the fender.

A newly re-styled V-8 emblem (compare page 151) now is used to mark the engine's selection.

A new delta-winged chromed ornament, differing from the swept-wing style used in 1953 (page 150) is now used on the hood.

Headlights are recessed, and the inner ring of the "door" is chromed.

This new stamped spinner is not pierced. What appears to be intake vents at the edges of the circle are merely painted sections of the single-piece stamping.

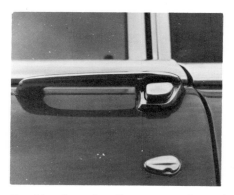

Outside door handles are unchanged from the type introduced in 1952.

Bright metal trim outlines all windows and the plastic insert of the Skyliner roof.

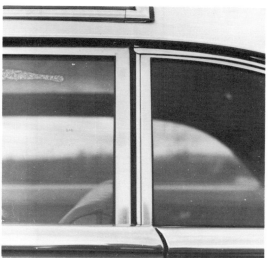

The self-edge framing of the windows provides a "pillar" when windows are up, but this disappears when windows are retracted.

The Crestline (or Customline, as appropriate) designation appears on the rear fenders just under the extended side trim. This side trim is omitted on the Mainline series, and Mainline name placed on the front fenders.

The rear fender is trimmed as shown on the Crestline series. The Customline and the Mainline series lack the three trailing "hash marks", but do have the single, larger, trim piece.

The 1954 tail light has a three-pointed, stylized, bright metal-like plastic insert placed over the lens, and an indented, and painted, pattern on the rim.

Unlike the 1953 style which had a pattern confined to its hub, the 1954 deck lid handle has these embossments on its ends.

The rear deck lid handle resembles the 1953 style; the key lock is built into its hub. Above the handle is the Ford crest framed in a chromed die casting.

The bumper guards are again restyled, and are designed to avoid locking with other bumpers.

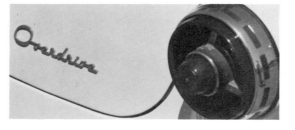

As appropriate, an Overdrive or a Fordomatic script is placed on the rear right deck lid if one of the accessory transmission is installed.

Other than the Mainline series, all cars have arm rests placed on the doors. The inside door handle is unchanged from the style presented first in 1951.

Upholstery of the door panels varies considerably with the Series. The special paneling of the Skyliner is an elaborate combination of two-tone vinyl and bright metal trim. The Mainline has a single-color vinyl.

Inside door lock knobs are plastic, even in the top of the line cars.

The data plate continues to be found on the left front door pillar.

Door latches are identical to the 1953 rotary lock. The insert is made of nylon, one of the earliest uses of the material in an automotive application.

A "flat" steering wheel presides over a re-styled instrument panel.

A half-circle horn ring is again provided. However, this is somewhat different in shape than the 1953 style with which it does not interchange.

The two-spoke steering wheel is available in colors to harmonize with the interiors. Mainline series had black only, and with no horn ring.

Power options introduced in the 1954 model included Master Guide power steering, and, when furnished, it was commemorated by the name cast into the horn ring.

A Ford crest is moulded into the plastic hub of the steering wheel of the Crestline and Customline cars. Mainline hub merely had a plain red rendition of the word Ford.

The 1954 speedometer reflected the current interest in greater horsepower, and presumably speed, as it showed a maximum index of 110 mph after years of 100 mph calibrations. Numerals are printed on clear plastic and seem suspended in space as they are back-lighted through a clear plastic transom placed on the top surface. The lights on either side at the bottom of the speedometer are green-lensed turn signal indicators.

Of the basic four instrument gauges, only two remain, that for fuel level, and radiator coolant temperature. The other two functions are taken over by lights which shine red to indicate low oil-pressure or non-charging of battery. At lower left is an air vent; on the right the blower switch for the Magic Aire Temperature System, now built into the panel not merely hung beneath.

Re-styled knobs appear on the instrument panel, but functions are relatively unchanged.

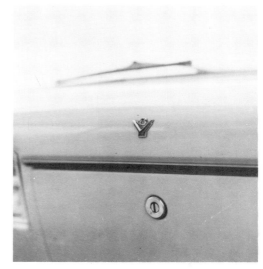

A locking parcel compartment is furnished and an optional interior light is available. The small V-8 on the instrument panel indicates engine selection as it has since 1952.

An ash tray is placed under the push button radio, and the radio speaker again returned to the top center of the panel where it had previously been located prior to 1951. To the right of the radio is an electric clock.

The view from the front seat of a Skyliner is unsurpassed. Whether clear, raining, night, or day, the effect is startling. No wind nois[e] intrude, inside all is quiet, conversation, a virtual impossibility in a Convertible when the top is down, is unaffected.

The Skyliner name was introduced with the 1954 model and then withdrawn, for although a similar model was continued in 195[5] and 1956, it did not bear that name, but was known simply as a modified Crown Victoria. During 1956 the "Bubbletop" was disco[n]tinued and the plastic-topped Ford was not again resumed for almost 20 years.

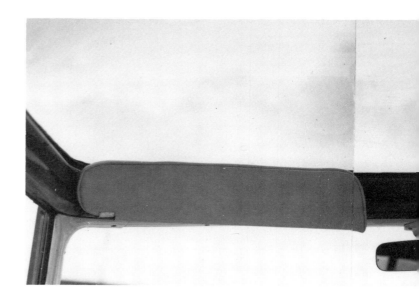

A ¼ inch tinted plastic panel is placed in a rubber gasket and surrounded by a bright metal trim strip.

The roof panel extends over the front seat and affords even the rear seat passengers an excellent view.

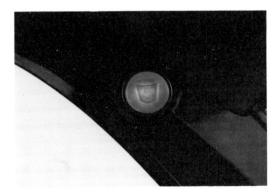

Interior lights are as introduced in 1952.

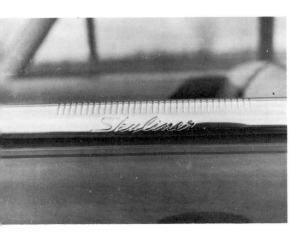

The treatment of the roof rear quarter is similar to the Victoria, but does differ. The cross-hatched gold plastic field with its Ford crest adds to the appearance of this area. The Victoria quarter (page 152) shows only bright metal with the crest in an embossed circle. The trim of the Skyliner above the rear window repeats a similar pattern to that found on the tail lights, while the Victoria is merely a grooved strip.

173

MAINLINE   **CUSTOMLINE**

FAIRLANE -- VICTORIA AND SUNLINER   **COUNTRY SQUIRE**

In the Fall of 1954, Ford introduced a new car, the Thunderbird, which is properly a subject of special interest. Volume #4 of this Series, entitled THUNDERBIRD!, describes the introduction of, and illustrates the subsequent history of that car. Readers are invited to consult THUNDERBIRD! for information on the car.

Y-Block V-8 Engine: 272 cu. in. displacement; overhead-valve, 90°-V type; 3.62 in. bore x 3.30 in. stroke; 5 main bearings; dual, downdraft carburetor. Dual exhaust system on Fairlane and Station Wagon models.

I-Block Six Engine: 223 cu. in. displacement; overhead-valve, in-line type; 3.62 in. bore x 3.60 in. stroke; 4 main bearings; unit-design, downdraft carburetor.

Engine Features: Deep-block construction; short-stroke, low-friction design; Automatic Power Pilot; turbo-wedge combustion chambers; 4-point suspension system; 3-ring super-fitted aluminum alloy pistons, rubber-floated vibration damper; free-turning intake and exhaust valves with integral guides and seats; precision-molded alloy iron crankshaft; high-lift, cast alloy camshaft with silent-chain drive. Full-pressure lubrication system; series-flow cooling system with positive-action thermostat. Six-volt starter-ignition system; low cut-in 35 amp. generator; high-torque starting motor, anti-kickout drive; weatherproof ignition system; special anti-fouling 18 mm spark plugs; 17-plate, 90 ampere-hour battery.

Semi-Centrifugal Clutch (with Conventional and Overdrive Transmissions): Dry, single-plate type; sintered bronze pilot bearing; ball-type throwout bearing; suspended pedal. 9.5 in. diameter pressure-plate with Six, 10 in. diameter with V-8.

Conventional Drive: Selective gear type, 3-speeds forward, 1 reverse; all gears helical type. Ratios (to 1); with Six engine, first 2.78, second 1.61, reverse 3.36; with V-8 engine, first 2.57, second 1.63, reverse 3.13.

Overdrive: 3-speed, selective-gear type transmission with planetary gear train providing automatic fourth gear (ratio 0.70 to 1); cuts in at 28 mph (approx.), cuts out at 22 mph (approx.).

Fordomatic: Torque converter type with automatic planetary gear train; single stage, 3-element, hydraulic torque converter; forced air cooling; no electrical or vacuum connections; illuminated Safety-Sequence Selector. Automatic "low-gear" starts with wide-open throttle; automatic intermediate gear. Oil level dip stick in engine compartment.

New Double-Drop Frames: 5 cross-member type; heavy box-section side rails; K-bar construction. Special frame construction on Victoria, Crown Victorias, Sunliner and Station Wagons.

New Angle-Poised Ball-Joint Front Suspension: Rubber-bushed, tilted, transverse link type with ball joints; tailored-to-weight coil springs with tubular shock absorbers; rubber-bushed, 3-piece ride stabilizer.

Variable Rate Rear Suspension: 5-leaf, semi-elliptic springs; rubber-bushed brackets and tension-type shackles; friction-control inserts between all leaves; diagonally mounted tubular hydraulic shock absorbers. Station wagons have 7-leaf, semi-elliptic springs with inserts between top 4 leaves.

Rear Axle: Semi-floating type with hypoid gears; pressed steel banjo-type housing. Station wagon axle has composite type housing. Ratios (to 1) with Conventional Drive: Sedans and Coupes, with V-8—3.78 std., 3.89 available; with Six—3.89 std., 4.11 available. Station wagons with V-8 or Six—4.09 std., 4.27 available. Ratios (to 1) with Overdrive: Sedans and Coupes, with V-8—3.89 std., 3.78 available; with Six—4.11 std., 3.89 available. Station wagons with V-8 or Six—4.27. Ratios (to 1) with Fordomatic and V-8 or Six; Sedans and Coupes—3.30 std., 3.55 available. Station wagons—3.54.

Steering System: Symmetrical linkage with spring-loaded ball stud in steering cross link; worm-and-roller type gear; anti-friction bearings in gear box and steering column. 25.3 to 1 over-all steering ratio; 18-in. dia. steering wheel; approximately 41-ft. turning diameter.

Hotchkiss Drive: Tubular propeller shaft; pre-lubricated needle bearings in universal joints.

New Hydraulic Brakes: Double-seal, 4-wheel duo-servo type; suspended pedal. 11 in. dia. composite drums; 192 sq. in. lining area on Sedans and Coupes, 202 sq. in. on Station Wagons.

Wheels and Tires: Super-balloon tubeless type tires with quiet high-traction treads. Mainline and Customline models and Fairlane Sedans—6.70 x 15 4-ply on 5-in. rims std. Sunliner, Victoria and Crown Victorias with Conventional or Overdrive transmissions—6.70 x 15 4-ply tires std.; with V-8 and Fordomatic—7.10 x 15 4-ply std. Ranch Wagons—7.10 x 15 4-ply tires std., 6-ply available. Country Sedans and Country Squire—7.10 x 15 6-ply tires std.

Exterior Dimensions: 115.5″ wheelbase; 58″ front and 56″ rear treads. Over-all width—75.9″; over-all length—station wagons 197.6″, all others 198.5″; over-all height (design load)—Tudor and Fordor models 61.0″; Victoria 60.1″; Crown Victoria 59.0″; Sunliner 58.9″; station wagons 62.2″.

Features—All Models: Astra-Dial Control Panel with ash tray; locking-type parcel compartment and illuminated controls; dual windshield wipers; double-swivel rear view mirror; 2-spoke steering wheel; interior light with manual switch; Automatic Posture Control front seat mechanism; non-sag seat construction; positive-action door stay checks, 2-position type on front doors; rotor-type door latches; safety-type inside push-button on rear doors of 4-door models; body ventilation air ducts with controls.

By 1955, manufacturers of the high-priced cars had developed their own euphemism for the car. In their vocabulary, "fine" was a substitute word for "quality" which in turn was another word for "high-priced". Ford then took direct aim on this high-priced, quality, luxury, market and described itself as indicated here.

The new Fairlane line (now replacing the Crestline series) was abundantly trimmed with luxury-appearing fabrics and nylon and vinyl. Metallic threads were woven into the closed car upholstery, and steering wheels and columns were color-matched to harmonize with the interiors. Wheelbase was increased slightly (to 115.5 inches) and a new concept of a luxury sports car called the Thunderbird was initially introduced at the top of the Fairlane line to add stature to the entire series. (The Thunderbird, so fundamentally different than the conventional passenger car, was promptly to be spun off into a new line of its own leaving only the reflected glory of its having initially been contemplated as the **senior** member of the Fairlane series).

Styling in the 1955 models is completely new, sharper, with straighter lines and sharper angles than before. This year saw the introduction of sharp new two-tone color schemes integrated (or rather split) at handsome new side trim lines rather than at the conventional base of the roof line. Wrapped-around windshields added to the modern appearance, and the performance of the two-speed Fordomatic was greatly improved by a redesign which enabled a "speed-trigger" start from low gear by sharply depressing the accelerator pedal (previously, Fordomatic units started only in intermediate gear). A new 272 c.i.d. Y-block engine now provided 160 horsepower against the 130 of the 1954 engine although HP ratings were now being minimized in favor of other design features.

Ford's 1955 Customline and Mainline series were reduced to two models in each line, a Fordor and a Tudor. Gone was the Coupe body style which last appeared in the similar lines of 1954. Henceforth the Business Coupe was to be merely a Mainline Tudor sedan with the omission of the rear seats.

Appointments, accessories, and details of the new Fairlane series were far more luxurious than anything previously and with this somewhat gaudy, yet utterly fascinating Series, Ford had **earned** the new designation that it had selected as "the fine car of its field".

BODY TYPES

70 B Mainline Tudor Sedan	60 B Fairlane Victoria	79 A Ranch Wagon
70 D Mainline Business Sedan	64 A Fairlane Crown-Victoria-solid top	59 B Custom Ranch Wagon
73 A Mainline Fordor Sedan	64 B Fairlane Crown Victoria-transparent top	79 B 8-Passenger Country Sedan
70 B Customline Tudor Sedan	73 C Fairlane Town Sedan (4-dr)	79 B 6-Passenger Country Sedan
73 B Customline Fordor Sedan	70 C Fairlane Club Sedan (2-dr)	79 C Country Squiare Station Wagon
	76 B Fairlane Convertible Coupe (Sunliner)	

1955 Type 60 B Fairlane Victoria

Mr. Len Barbieri, San Diego, California

The Victoria features the "pillar-less" visibility resulting from having the window trim retract with the glass.

After four years of use, the familiar Ford crest has been restyled sharply, and now bears a crown effect.

The rear window now has a different intersection with the roof quarter (page 173) and there is no dress-up trim of the corner post as previously.

The new rectangular vent window has been narrowed almost to the length of the locking arm.

A major change is the wrap-around windshield which now intrudes into the area formerly occupied by the triangular vent window.

The Fairlane series is the top of the 1955 line and its trim is special and unique. The Customline and Mainline cars share the body shell, but not the trim.

The chromed trim piece on the headlight door is exclusively 1955 Fairlane. It was not used on any other car.

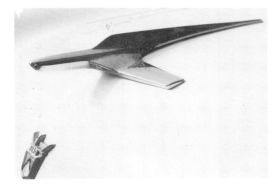

The new chromed hood ornament is used on all three series in the 1955 line.

A re-styled Ford Crest (compare page 150) is used on the front of the hood of the Fairlane series. The earlier style crest continues to be used on Customline and Mainline. Beneath the Crest on the Fairlane only appears its name.

At both ends of the new rectangular-pierced grill, and under the headlights, are the parking lights.

These large round parking lights are used only in 1955.

1955 saw the start of a re-direction of Ford's attention to the matter of Safety. Among the subtle changes in their cars were the incorporation of a double-swiveled rear view mirror which would move out of the way when hit.

The new windshield wraps around the corner and the corner post is moved back into a vertical position.

The data plate is placed on the cowl directly beneath the windshield where it can be seen when the door is opened.

The bumper guards are similar in appearance to the 1954 style but do not interchange.

Resembling the earlier style, the 1955 rotary door latch is secured with three screws rather than two as on the 1954 style (page 169).

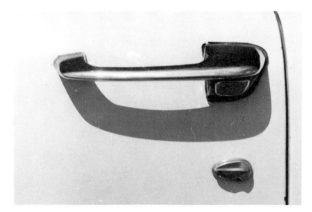

Standard hardware such as the outside door locks and handles continue unchanged from previous years.

As previously, door locks come in pairs. They are installed with their notched edge facing downwards to avoid collecting moisture.

Inside door lock knobs on all series are plastic. A rubber grommet lines the hole in the sill to protect the base of the grommet.

The window handles are replaced with switches when the optional power windows (introduced on the 1954 model) are used.

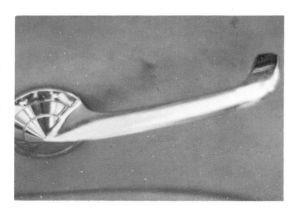

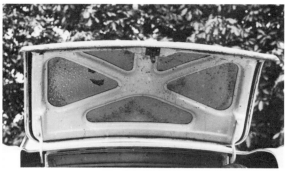

The wide rear deck lid opens to a large deep luggage compartment. The spare wheel is mounted vertically at the right.

A new rotary deck latch appears for the first time.

The center-fill fuel tank is continued, and it passes through the luggage compartment briefly. A new latch plate is used with the rotary latch.

The new Fairlane Crest, the nameplate, and a chromed casting trim placed at the lower edge of the rear deck lid are three of the items that are exclusively Fairlane trim in 1955.

The license plate bracket is hinged at its lower edge to permit access to the concealed tube cap.

The Fordomatic or Overdrive nameplates continue to be used to designate optional transmission choices.

The 1955 Tail Light is built into the fender, but lowered from its position at the top in 1954, to allow for the installation of back-up lights as shown here.

When the optional, extra-cost back up lights are not ordered, a corrugated bright metal trim plate conceals the opening.

The exclusive Fairlane side trim which begins atop the headlight and runs to the rear at the side of the car (lower right corner of photo) is joined by a second trim strip at the crown of the rear fenders terminating at the back of the fender.

A clear plastic insert in the housing above the speedometer illuminates the dial.

The steering wheel is available in either black or white. As before, Mainline series does not have the horn ring.

The horn button on the Fairlane and Customline series has the Ford crest. If power steering option is installed, the name is spaced at the circumference of the button.

To the right of the fuel level gauge is an OIL light which glows red in the event of low pressure.

A Generator light glows red in the event of loss of charging circuit. The temperature guage reads "H" when off, a confusing condition that was shortly corrected.

These controls are to the left of the steering column on the instrument panel.

The parking brake handle is suspended below the instrument panel.

Contemporary interest in horsepower and speed is translated into the speedometer for 1955 which now reads to a maximum of 120 miles per hour. In the two years since the introduction of the overhead valve engine in 1954, rated horsepower had almost doubled, and although manufacturers were soft-pedaling their claims (in fact, horsepower was one of the specifications NOT advertised in 1955) in favor of things like style, safety features, appearance, etc., the fact remains that the cars were now comfortably capable of cruising at ten or fifteen miles per hour faster.

The Fordomatic position indicator has been placed on the instrument panel at the base of the steering column. When not installed, this opening is covered by a blanking plate.

Ford's Magic Aire System has a new control head, built into the instrument panel, and containing controls for combined heating, defrosting, and ventilating.

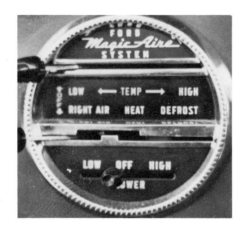

The new Super Range radio is a seven-tube radio with five-station push button tuning. A lower-priced five-tube radio is an alternate option.

The optional electric clock matches in appearance the other two instruments as does the standard (except for Mainline) 30 hour stem wind clock.

A new option this year is the Automatic Choke which does away with hand-choking the engine. In place of the choke knob (below), a blanking plate is placed in the dashboard in its place.

Two characteristic crimped rings appear at the base of the passenger car radio antenna.

Under the instrument panel, on the firewall, is a duct for the heater and in-coming air. A flap is placed in this duct to divert part of the air to the passenger's side of the car.

The V-8 engine selection insignia has been placed on the glove box cover, and the latch formerly on the cover has been moved to the instrument panel above it.

Not only is the Fairlane line new in 1955, but the Town Sedan is a new name given to the top-of-the-line four door sedan. Like other models in the Fairlane series, it is specially trimmed and appointed.

1955 Type 73 C Fairlane Town Sedan

Mr. Sam Williamson, Oceanside, California

For convenience in entering, both doors are hinged at the front.

The dome light in the Town Sedan has a self-contained ON/OFF switch but it is also controlled by switches in the front doors.

The trim above the rear window differs from that used on the Fairlane Victoria (page 178).

Rear doors are faired into the window corner posts for best effect.

In addition to the well-known "Fairlane" side trim which sweeps along the sides of the car, additional bright metal trim at the base of the windows continues along the top of the rear fenders to the tail light.

The Town Sedan nameplate appears on the rear fenders.

After offering power windows on the 1946 and 1947 Sportsman, Ford discarded the system and it was not again offered until re-introduced in 1954. When employed, a master panel appeared on the left front door to operate *all* windows, and individual switches (below right) appeared at the other locations.

The Fairlane Town Sedan door panels have a distinctive trim pattern. Upholstery is done in metallic-threaded nylon materials with two-tone interiors the rule. Seats are done in random-twist nylon and the bolsters (top portion) are pleated. Arm rests are placed on all four doors.

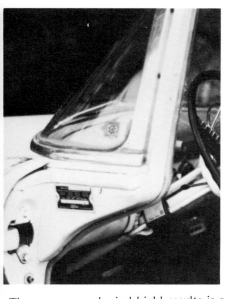

The wrap-around windshield results is a "dog-legged" effect below the windshield. Attractive when the door is closed, the appearance of the protruding corner does not invite entry.

1955 Type 73 B Customline Fordor Sedan

Resembling the Fairlane at first glance, the hood of the other lines lacks the Fairlane script beneath the Crest.

Sharing a body with the Fairlane series, the Customline is less heavily trimmed. For example, the windshield post on the front doors are not trimmed.

There is no stripe along the top of the rear fenders as there is on the Fairlane series.

The tail lights on the Customline are identical with those on the Fairlane.

A different Crest appears on the rear deck lid as a part of the lock. Compare with page 182 for appearance of the Fairlane.

Headlight "doors" on the Customline and Mainline series are not trimmed with the chromed strip on their upper lip (page 179). They are otherwise interchangeable.

The optional transmission choice is again advertised with the placement of its name on the right rear corner of the deck lid. The chromed trim that appears at the bottom edge of the Fairlane deck lid (page 182) is omitted on the other lines.

Type 70 B Mainline Tudor Sedan

Mr. Oliver Himiston, San Diego, California

The Mainline Tudor sedan is a six passenger sedan offered at the economy end of the scale. It follows Ford's custom of less-heavily trimming such cars and like most of them, it lacks added niceties including horn rings, second sun visor, arm rests, and so on.

The 1955 Tudor sedan is a departure in that for the first time there is no true coupe model and the Type 70 D Mainline Business Sedan is a variant of the Tudor. Popular with Fleet-type applications where a three-passenger car is adequate, and where storage space is desirable, the Business Sedan is identical to the Tudor except that the entire rear seat assembly is omitted and the compartment merely paneled.

No trim strip appears on the sides of the Mainline

Ford's six cylinder engine has been selected for this car.

Rear window of the Mainline series lacks the bright metal trim of the other lines.

Windshield of the Mainline is trimmed in rubber and lacks the brightwork of the other lines.

1955 Type 79 C Country Squire Station Wagon

The Country Squire was the top-of-the-line station wagon offering some degree of luxury and appearance in addition to utility. Its rear seat cushion and back were removeable and the center seat could be folded flat to provide ample cargo space easily entered from the rear tailgate. The center seat is divided so that the smaller section nearer the curb could be folded separately to allow entry to the rear seat.

The body is all-steel and the "wooden" panels are merely decals applied directly over the steel. The mouldings around the panels are fiber-glass with attractive chrome-headed fittings. The headlights, since the model is reflective of the Fairlane, bear the chrome trim (page 179), but the hood ornament is the conventional Ford crest.

The Type 79 A Ranch Wagon is a two-door economy entry into the station wagon series. Lacking a third seat, it is modestly trimmed, but does have a chrome side stripe.

196

Growing in popularity is the all-metal Country Sedan model which is essentially the same as the Country Squire but which lacks the "wooden" side trim and some of the dress-up features of the Fairlane series. In its 8-passenger form it is trimmed with the "Fairlane" stripe as shown here. An alternate model has no third seat and a second seat that is not split for access to the rear. It is known as a "6-passenger Country Sedan" and while similar in other respects, lacks the side trim.

1955 Type 79 B Country Sedan   Mr. Henry Pohl, Oceanside, California

The interior door panels of the Country Sedan bear a distinctive two-tone color scheme reminiscent of the "Fairlane stripe", the chrome stripe on the sides of the passenger cars of that series.

The all-metal bodies of the Country Sedans were promoted as "requiring no maintenance" referring to the need for protection of the earlier wooden station wagon bodies.

A rotary latch and chromed outside handle secures the lift-gate at the rear.

Rear quarter windows slide open, and an inside catch is provided for protection.

Special spring-loaded counter balanced hinges are used to hold the lift-gate open.

A two-color vinyl upholstery is installed in the Country Sedan. This is the second seat of the six-passenger model.

The seat cushion is hinged at its front lower edge to pivot upward, and the seat back then rotates forward to add to the cargo carrying space in the Country Sedan.

Two collapsible-type hinges support the tail gate to add an additional load space.

The spare tire is carried beneath a hinged flap in the floor of the rear compartment.

"The Fine Car at Half the Fine Car Price"

MAINLINE

CUSTOMLINE

FAIRLANE -- VICTORIA AND SUNLINER

COUNTRY SQUIRE

1956 was a year of some consequential improvements in the Ford cars. A 12 volt ignition system ended starting problems, and a brand new model, the Fordor Victoria was introduced along with some higher horsepower engines and still higher optional engines. The factory offered an accessory built-in air conditioner (with vents arranged around the dash-mounted radio speaker), some "exquisite new fabrics", and a 9-tube "Signal Seek" radio.

The Thunderbird had been well-received and had achieved the prestige position it was intended for so the spill-over of derivitive characteristics was well-regarded. Among these was the designation of the new 292 cid engine as the "Thunderbird" Y-8 Special engine and the advertisement of the engine by the use of a stylized Thunderbird insignia on the front fender of the Fairlane series. The Customline and the Mainline series used the 272 cid engine of 1955 and bore a V-8 insignia in place of the Thunderbird on their fender (unless the Six was ordered).

The big effort of 1956 though was an offering of "Lifeguard" safety features. Having discarded the term after first using it to describe the 1949 chassis, Ford bowed to what is now considered a matter of "public demand", and reported on a study by the Automobile Safety Research group at Cornell University. This had disclosed that the three major causes of injuries in automotive accidents were (1) occupants thrown from the car, (2) passengers striking the windshield or instrument panel, and (3) driver thrown against the steering wheel. Ford's solutions, offered amidst some low-keyed promotion, were (1) improved door locks plus optional seat belts, (2) double-swiveled rear view mirrors, and optional padded dashboard covers and sun visors, and (3) a deep-dished steering wheel.

With the standard items and the addition of some of the optional accessories only a few of which are mentioned here, Ford had a right to its claim for the 1956 models as "the fine car at half the fine car price!".

BODY TYPES

57 A Fairlane Fordor Victoria	64 D Customline Victoria	59 A Ranch Wagon
64 A Fairlane Crown Victoria (solid top)	70 B Customline Tudor Sedan	59 B Custom Ranch Wagon
64 B Fairlane Crown Victoria (transparent top)	73 B Customline Fordor Sedan	59 C Parklane Ranch Wagon
64 C Fairlane Victoria		
70 C Fairlane Club Sedan	70 A Mainline Tudor Sedan	79 B 8-passenger Country Sedan
73 C Fairlane Town Sedan	70 D Mainline Business Sedan	79 C Country Squire
76 B Fairlane Convertible Coupe	73 A Mainline Fordor Sedan	79 D 6-passenger Country Sedan

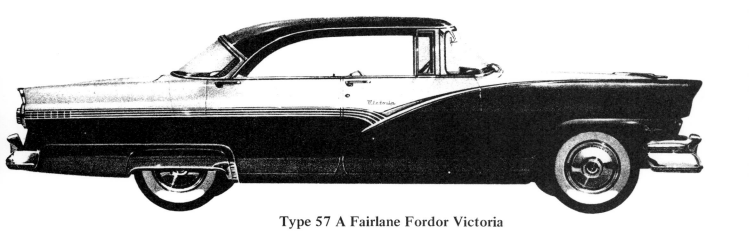

Type 57 A Fairlane Fordor Victoria

1956 Type 76B Fairlane Convertible Coupe

The Convertible Coupe, also known as the "Sunliner", like the Country Squire, represents the penultimate in the Ford line. Enhanced with the most attractive trim, equipped with the most lavish appointments, strikingly styled, these cars were most popular with the Country Club set.

Mr. William Isenhouer, La Jolla, California

The wide plastic rear window had been introduced in 1950 and has continued on the Convertibles ever since.

The Fairlane trim special for 1956 includes a stripe which commences atop the headlight door. No trim is used on its forward lip as was done in 1955. (page 179)

The re-styled hood ornament is a chromed die casting.

The Fairlane Crest, with its extended points, surmounts the name on the front of the hood.

The passenger car version of the Thunderbird insignia is this one which is used on the fenders of the Fairlane series and the station wagons only. It signifies the choice of the Thunderbird Y-8, a 292 cid, 4-barrel carburetor, dual exhaust engine with automatic choke and a 202 horsepower rating.

Parking lights have been reduced in size and are now more elliptical than round.

Greatly resembling the stripe on the side of the 1955 Fairlane model (page 176), the 1956 version dips sharply at the center.

The windshield area is little changed from 1955, and the same rectangular vent window is used.

The model name appears near the dip in the trim at the side of the car as it did in 1955, but the engine identification insignia has been moved to the front fender.

As previously, a data plate is affixed to the dog-legged section of the cowl at the left side of the car.

Fender shields are a heavily-promoted extra-cost item that is frequently found on the extravagantly trimmed Fairlane series. They are styled to harmonize with the existing standard quarter panel trim plate.

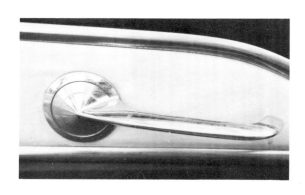

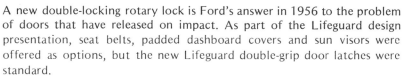

A new double-locking rotary lock is Ford's answer in 1956 to the problem of doors that have released on impact. As part of the Lifeguard design presentation, seat belts, padded dashboard covers and sun visors were offered as options, but the new Lifeguard double-grip door latches were standard.

The wide Breezeway rear window can be unzipped for ventilation.

Two chromed latches at the header secure it to the windshield frame.

Snaps are provided at its base for the boot which is installed over a folded top.

The strap metal frame of the top is painted, not chromed.

Ash trays are provided in the arm rests for the rear seat passengers.

The Fairlane crest is placed decoratively in the center of the rear seat back.

A sharply pointed insignia appears on the rear deck of the Fairlane models.

A simulated "exhaust" appears in the pattern of the side trim. On the Fairlane models, an additional trim extends from the base of the windows along the top of the rear fenders.

A bright plastic trim is installed over the tail light lens.

Back-up lights, optional extra cost accessories are installed just above the tail light in a location otherwise fitted with a metal blanking plate.

The ends of the bumper are pierced to allow passage from the new dual exhaust system, standard on both V-8 engine choices.

All instruments are grouped under a shroud formed by the instrument panel. Green-lensed lights above the speedometer indicate turn signal operation.

The optional Fordomatic transmission lever position is displayed on an indicator at the base of the steering column.

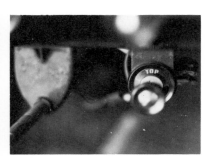

This knob, suspended beneath the instrument panel to the left of the steering column, operates the power system to retract the Convertible top.

Although 1956 Mainline and Customline models had black steering wheels, color was introduced in the Fairlanes. Wheels installed to harmonize with the interiors included Green, Gray, Orange (in Victoria and Sunliner) and Raven Black.

Ford's Lifeguard Safety Program was enhanced by this new steering wheel, the first *basic* change in years. The hub of the wheel has been recessed by the use of upward-pointing spokes to reduce the danger of injury if the driver were to be thrown against it as in impact. The horn ring has also been recessed in a similar manner.

As in 1955, the ends of the gear shift lever (and the turn signal, when installed) are oval-shaped black plastic knobs.

The hub of the steering wheel is fitted with a plastic-moulded Ford crest, a variation of the past designs. If the Master Guide power steering option was installed, its name would appear, cast into the metal hub, at its circumference.

1956 saw the efforts by Ford to market "safety" as a commodity with less than spectacular results. The results of a study made at Cornell University were widely reported and Ford, believing that the Public would receive safety-oriented improvements with enthusiasm introduced several. The results of their efforts are in many ways long-lasting, but at the time were accepted only with apparent indifference.

Among the items (safety belts, improved door locks, and the deep-center steering wheel were the others) was an option which covered padded sun visors and a padded instrument panel cover.

Under the covers, however, was the all-metal painted instrument panel. The one seen on this page is typical of by far the most popular as Ford sold relatively few of the padded covers.

All instruments are black-faced with red-tipped indicator needles and are set into a painted panel. The temperature guage reads "H" in its off position and does not here indicate an abnormality. Red warning lights are joined to form a dual-gauge for oil pressure-and-charge indicator.

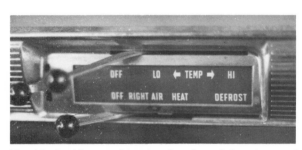

The Magic Aire combination heating, defrosting, and ventilating system control head is built into the panel, below and to the right, of the clock.

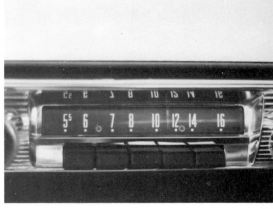

Ford's new Signal-Seek Radio, a high fidelity type with nine tubes became available in 1956. A feature of this radio is the choice of T (town) or C (country) sensitivity in stations seeking.

The Ford Console Range radio is a six-tube push button radio. Both this radio and the Signal Seek (above) have the civil defense Conelrad tuning mark on their dials.

A locking latch is provided for the glove compartment which now slopes forward and downwards to contain small items better. The script on the panel is omitted on the Mainline series.

956 Type 64 A Fairlane Crown Victoria (solid top)   Mr. Howard Lampke, Orange, California

956 Type 64 B Fairlane Crown Victoria (transparent top)   Mr. John Baum, Westminster, California

The 1956 side trim dips near the center of the door both on the two-and on the four-door models.

Victorias were popular and accordingly they commanded a large segment of Ford's line. There was the four-door Victoria, newly introduced in 1956, the earlier two-door (first introduced in 1951), the Crown Victoria in two versions, and even a Customline Victoria which was less popular, possibly because it had less flashy trim than the Fairlane model.

Door panels feature longer streamlined arm rests, and a specially prepared vinyl covering embossed in a rectangular pattern.

One of the more curious of several Ford innovations is the Crown Victoria produced only
in 1955 and 1956. Despite its excellent trim
and special sales-inducing extras (such as a rear
seat fold-up arm rest), it negated the very
essence of the Victoria's interest by raising a
pillar of chrome behind the door and up and
over the top.

In a further modification of a design, Ford
offered that same Crown Victoria with its forward roof section replaced by a plastic panel.
Its effect was similar to 1954's Skyliner, a name
that was not extended to this model.

A chromed pillar rises just ahead of
the rear windows and extends across
the top.

The rear edge of the "crown" contains a familar
pattern of rectangular embossments painted to suggest ventilation exhaust.

215

The appearance from the windshield back to the interior trim strip presents a conventional appearance in the Crown Victoria (solid top).

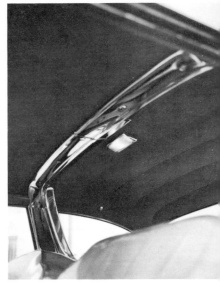

The interior of both Crown Victorias is embellished with a wide trim strip matching the course of the outer trim.

Interior light is supplied by this lamp placed just behind the trim strip.

The Crown Victoria with the transparent top is furnished with a fabric shade that is zippered on three sides. It may be folded back and stuffed behind the interior trim piece (center photo). Either side may be released independently.

Both Crown Victorias (and *only* these models) have a fold-up center arm rest in the rear seat.

The spare wheel is contained in a well at the right side of the luggage compartment. A wing nut and spacer placed over a hinged threaded shaft hold the wheel securely.

1956 Type 70 C Fairlane Club Sedan

Mr. Arthur Jamison, Oceanside, California

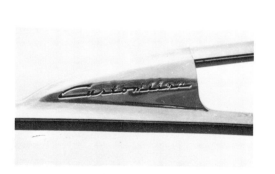

Customline and Mainline cars received the earlier, 176 hp 272 cid engine when V-8 was selected. This insignia then appeared on the front fender in place of the one exclusively marking the 292 cid Thunderbird special engine (page 204).

1956 Type 70 B Customline Tudor Sedan

Wheel covers are incorrect

The conventional 1956 Fairlane trim stripe appears on the sides of the Fairlane Club Sedan.

The Club Sedan and the Tudors share a body style in which the window pillars appear, even with the windows retracted.

Fender shields are optional dress-up extra cost accessories. Although generally found on the Fairlane models, they are less frequently seen on Customline and Mainline cars.

Ford's new "Lifeguard" double-swivel mirror moves easily out of the way on impact.

The upholstery design of the doors on the Customline differ from that used on the Fairlane series (page 206).

Fairlane and Customline cars have arm rests on the doors, but the Mainline series does not.

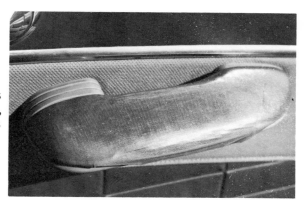

1956 Type 73 C Fairlane Town Sedan

A complete new 12 volt electrical system was presented on all cars in the line for 1956. This included the battery, generator, regulator, all lights, radio, etc. None of these parts will interchange with the earlier six volt system.

The dual tailpipes of the Thunderbird Special V-8 in the Fairlane models are routed through the rear bumpers, but the smaller V-8 option in the Customline or Mainline series is fitted with a cross-over pipe and those cars have only one conventional exhaust.

Unlike the Victorias, the Town Sedan does not have a stripe at the top of its rear fenders (page 208).

While the 1955 Fairlane stripe was an unbroken line, the 1956 style appears to be the sum of two separate curves meeting at the center of the front door.

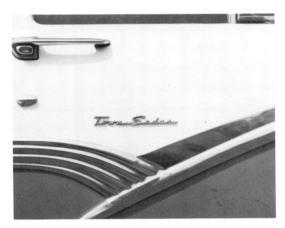

The Town Sedan name is nicely framed by the juncture of the stripe sections on the door.

Town Sedans, unlike Victorias, do not have the bright metal trim at the base of the windows.

1956

1956 Type 73 A Mainline Fordor Sedan

The Ford crest on the hood of the Mainline series is the earlier style. The crowned Crest (page 204) is reserved for use on the Fairlane series.

Initially built with no rear quarter side trim, the Mainline cars were soon given a single stripe with the fancy forward plate; two tone cars were built with a second stripe below the first and the enclosed area correspondingly painted as shown above.

The Mainline, like the Customline series had two V-8 options, but only of the Ford 272 or Thunderbird 292 cid engines (the big 312 was reserved for the Fairlane series). Either V-8 engine in the Mainline is marked by this V-8 insignia.

The horn button on the Mainline (there is no horn ring) is relatively plain compared to the upper-line cars (page 210).

Tail light housings interchange with the others in the model year, but the Mainline back-up light frame is painted instead of chromed.

56 Type 59 C Parklane Ranch Wagon

The window pillar and door jam are trimmed with a chrome trim unique to this model

A luxury model, the Parklane had the Fairlane-type stripe on its side and atop its rear fender.

Following Ford's custom of utilizing earlier designs, the Station Wagon line, including the ultra-fashion Parklane, are fitted with 1955 style back-up light housings.

ddition to two Ranch Wagons, and the four Country Sedans and Country Squire, in 1955 introduced the luxuriously appointed two door lane, an upgrading of the Ranch Wagon. With eting instead of rubber mats, special appearance s, and a vinyl cover to snap over the entire rear partment at the base of the windows, the model a "Fairlane" approach to the two-door station n market.

✱FAIRLANE SERIES

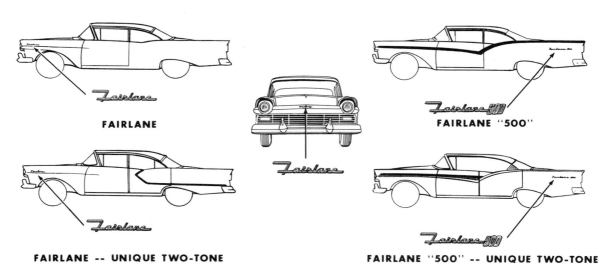

FAIRLANE

FAIRLANE "500"

FAIRLANE -- UNIQUE TWO-TONE

FAIRLANE "500" -- UNIQUE TWO-TONE

✱CUSTOM SERIES

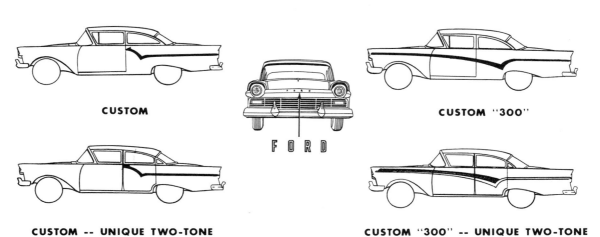

CUSTOM

CUSTOM "300"

CUSTOM -- UNIQUE TWO-TONE

CUSTOM "300" -- UNIQUE TWO-TONE

✱STATION WAGONS, ETC.

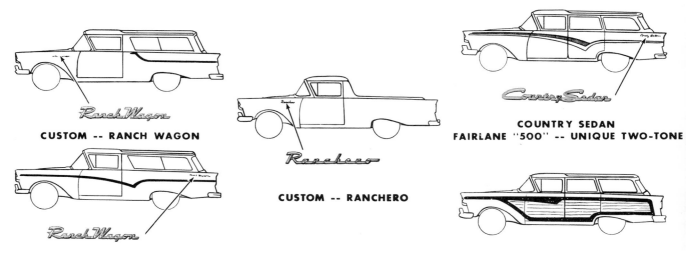

CUSTOM -- RANCH WAGON

CUSTOM -- RANCHERO

COUNTRY SEDAN
FAIRLANE "500" -- UNIQUE TWO-TONE

RANCH WAGON
CUSTOM "300" -- UNIQUE TWO-TONE

COUNTRY SQUIRE
FAIRLANE "500" -- UNIQUE TWO-TONE

✱ **Does not include all body types. Illustrations are representative models.**

51 A	Fairlane 500 Skyliner
57 A	Fairlane 500 Town Victoria
58 A	Fairlane 500 Town Sedan
63 A	Fairlane 500 Club Victoria
64 B	Fairlane 500 Club Sedan
76 B	Fairlane 500 Convertible Coupe
57 B	Fairlane Town Victoria
55 A	Fairlane Town Sedan
63 B	Fairlane Club Victoria
64 A	Fairlane Club Sedan

1957 Type 63 A Fairlane 500 Club Victoria

1957 saw the introduction of completely restyled cars bearing only a familiar resemblence to the earlier models. The new Fairlane series (which included two lines, the Fairlane 500 and the Fairlane) was some five inches lower than the 1956 Fords, had 2.5 inch longer wheelbases (118" vs 115.5") and an overall length of 207.7 inches, over nine inches longer. The Custom series which includes the Custom 300 and the Custom is built on chasis having a 116" wheelbase, one half inch longer than in 1956 and are but six inches shorter than the Fairlane models. They too are lower, by four inches, than the 1956 models. Gone is the Mainline Series as a name although the Custom has essentially replaced it. As an aid to lowering the cars, all had 14" wheels for the first time.

Other design changes include a front-hinged, rear-opening hood (for added safety in the unlikely event that the mechanical latch fails) with a return of the inside hood release knob, streamlined wheel openings, and fenders which continue forward to provide visors over the headlights. In addition, the windshield posts slope backward with a resultant curiously shaped vent window. Bumpers on the Fairlane Series are more massive and sweep further around the corners of the car.

The big news though for 1957 was the introduction of the Skyliner [first shown at the N.Y.C. Auto Show late in 1956] the name had been used before in 1954 for the transparent topped-Victoria). The 1957 Skyliner was an all-steel hardtop that was capable of changing into an open convertible at the touch of a button. An automatic folding mechanism retracted its top into the rear deck providing indisputable evidence for the claim of "A new kind of Ford for 1957".

1957 Type 63 B Fairlane Club Victoria

1957 Type 73 D Custom 300 Fordor Sedan

1957 Type 70 A Custom Tudor Sedan

70 B	Custom 300 Tudor Sedan
73 B	Custom 300 Fordor Sedan
70 A	Custom Tudor Sedan
70 D	Custom Business Tudor
73 A	Custom Fordor Sedan
59 A	Ranch Wagon
59 B	Del Rio Ranch Wagon
79 A	6 passenger Country Sedan
79 B	9 passenger Country Sedan
79 E	9 passenger Country Squire
66 A	Ranchero
66 B	Custom Ranchero

1957 Type 76 B Fairlane 500 Convertible Coupe

The "Sunliner", a generic name Ford had first used in 1953 to describe its Convertible Coupe continues as the high point in the Ford line. With an overall length of 207.7 inches (over 17 **feet**) it was some **nine inches longer** than the 1956 model, and with its smaller 14" tires and other design changes, it was almost 2½ inches lower as well.

Top up or top down, the sporty Sunliner attracts attention. Fairlane 500 styling stripes on its sides emphasize the long, low look, and the new rear-sloping windshield posts give added emphasis to the overall sleek look of the 1957 Convertible.

Mr. George Barlow, Fullerton, California

The Sunliner's top is power-operated by a combination electric motor-hydraulic oil pump located beneath the rear seat. The output of the pump is routed to two hydraulic cylinders, one at each side of the top in the well. These collapse or erect the folding top mechanism on command of an electric switch located beneath the instrument panel. Two over-center toggle latches on the front header secure the top to catches placed at the top of the windshield.

A greatly simplified hood ornament adds quiet elegance to the 1957 Ford.

The Fairlane Crest is placed in the hood ornament on all models.

The Fairlane name, in script, appears on the hood of the Fairlane 500 and Fairlane lines.

This elaborate side trim is unique to the Fairlane 500 series.

A restyled bumper guard harmonizes with the new wide front grill.

Front fenders on all models are extended to provide a hood over the headlights.

Rectangular parking lights are set into the front grill beneath the headlights.

A new windshield design for 1957 wraps the glass further around the corner (compare 1956 style page 205) and slopes the pillar to the rear.

Because of the rear-sloped pillar, the vent window takes on a new shape.

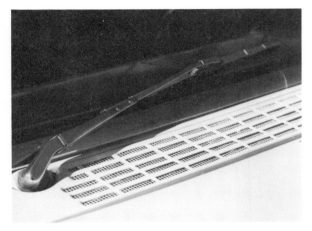

An intake at the base of the windshield is for the new cowl ventilation system.

The inside door lock knob is placed at the front of the door directly behind the vent window latch.

The new oval-based radio antenna is more streamlined than the earlier, round, style.

The top folds lower into a deeper well and a boot is again provided to cover the folded top.

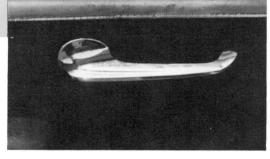

Newly re-styled inside door handles and window cranks add to the newness of the 1957 Ford.

The outside door handle is unchanged.

The data plate has been returned to the left front door pillar.

The "Fairlane" Crest appears at the center of the rear seat.

The seats of the 1957 Sunliner are upholstered to suggest "bucket" seats, a concession to contemporary interest in sports cars.

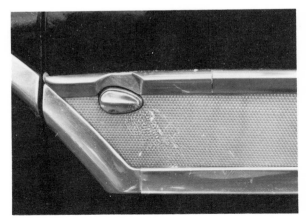

The side stripe, unique to the Fairlane 500 series, diminishes the appearance of the keylock.

A new Fairlane crest is applied at the center of the rear deck lid.

New massive wrap-around bumpers dip sharply at the center to accommodate the license plate and fuel filler tube. For the first time, no separate bumper guards are furnished.

The new "Hi-Canted" rear fender fin and "Jet-Tube" tail light represent Ford's maximum excursion into the somewhat unreal world of excessively high "tail fins" currently being offered by other manufacturers. In the words of one former employee "A high point of the 50's was Ford's admirable **restraint** *in the use of fins".*

The Fairlane 500 name appears in script on the rear fender.

Turn signals are standard starting in 1957, but back-up lights are an option which call for the substitution of an all-red lens (page 250) with this one which has an integral light at its center. The chromed trim at the top and trailing edge of the fenders is exclusively Fairlane 500 style.

The Ford crest appears at the center of the steering wheel.

Colors used in 1957 steering wheels include tan, green, dark ray metallic, and black.

The speedometer continues to show a maximum 120 mph indication, and the temperature gauge has been corrected to indicate "C" when off (page 212).

The gear shift lever knob is black.

Chromed top-mechanism knob is suspended beneath the instrument panel.

The control head for the Magic Aire system is built into the panel and features a small illuminated sub-panel for fan motor indication. For the first time the control for the incoming air is *not* on this panel, but placed in its initial position on the instrument panel (photo below).

This insignia on the glove box door refers to the selection of the 245 horsepower Thunderbird Special 312 cid V-8 engine (as opposed to the 212 hp Thunderbird 292).

A glove compartment at the right side of the instrument panel is secured by a lock placed within a crest-shaped escutcheon plate.

Right side incoming air is adjusted by a knob on the instrument panel.

The rarely used pedal on the right indicates a power brake used with a manual transmission (clutch pedal at left). Insert shows a non-power brake pedal as used with the Fordomatic transmission.

238

A transistor-powered Signal-Seek radio automatically tunes to all stations regardless of the direction in which the pointer is moving. With nine tubes, one of which operates the automatic tuning circuit, it has enough sensitivity to justify the (T) local station or country (C) choices. The speaker is located in the top center of the instrument panel above and slightly to the left of the radio.

A self-regulating clock re-adjusts its rate with each use of the time-setting stem in order to compensate for operating too fast or too slow. Like the other instruments, the clock dial is illuminated at night.

1957 Type 64 B Fairlane 500 Club Sedan

Mr. Tom Howard, Buena Park, California

The windows of the Club Sedan retract but the slender pillars do not.

A subtle difference exists in the trim on the rear roof pillar between the Club sedan and the Club Victoria (opposite page).

1957 Type 63 B Fairlane Club Victoria

Mr. Bill Anderson, Granada Hills, California

Other than the external side trim, the Fairlane 500 Club Victoria (Type 63 A) greatly resembles the lower-priced Fairlane model.

'airlane'' appears on the front nder.

1957 Type 57 A Fairlane 500 Town Victoria

Mr. Hugo Barbiera, Canoga Park, Californ

Introduced in the 1956 model year, the Town Victoria is a popular four door sedan with exceptionally sporty lines.

This view of the four door Town Victoria resembles that of the two door Club Victoria (previous page).

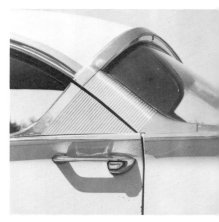

The rear door is framed into the quarter pillar and a bright metal trim affixed to it which is a major departure from the appearance of the two door version (opposite page). The roof slants out over the rear window in a visor effect similar to that in front.

1957 Type 63 A Fairlane 500 Club Victoria   Mr. Don Norem, Oceanside, California

The 1957 roof extends over the windshield in a visor effect.

The rear quarter pillar of the two door Victoria is slender and unlike the similiar view of a four door model.

The inside door panel of the Club Victoria is upholstered in white skivar grain vinyl, heat embossed with a rectangular pattern.

The front seat is adjusted by releasing this knob at the drivers left. 4-Way Power Front Seat is available as an optional extra cost accessory for powered adjustment of both fore-and-aft and also up-and-down.

1957 Type 70 A Custom Tudor Sedan

The name F-O-R-D appears just below the hood on the front of the Custom 300 and the Custom models.

The distinctive trim pattern at the rear quarter offers an excellent basis for the two-toning of 1957 Custom cars.

*Of the innovative ideas that Ford pursued, perhaps the most interesting of all was that of the Skyliner, a **true** "Hardtop Convertible". The entire roof section of this car would automatically remove and store itself in the rear compartment enabling snug weathertight coupe to be changed into an open air Convertible at will. Limited only by the increased cost and the obvious lack of storage with the top retracted, the Skyliner was to live a short manufacturing existence.*

1957 Type 51 A Fairlane 500 Skyliner

The Skyliner name appears at the base of the roof quarter in distinctive script.

The Skyliner bears a general resemblance to the Club Victoria window treatment.

A parting line appears across the roo just above the vent window.

Mr. Jim Hawtree, Lemon Grove, California

Due to a higher rear quarter section, the side trim on the Skyliner differs from that on the Fairlane 500 and the keylock falls in a different place in the pattern (page 235).

Fairlane crowned Crest appears just orward of the Skyliner name on the ase of the roof quarter.

The rear end and deck lid is higher than the same area of the Sunliner Convertible (page 236).

At 210.8 inches overall length, the Skyliner was over 3 inches *longer* than the Fairlane 500 series.

1957

Skyliner Exteriors: There are 12 new body colors available in Sin[g]
Color and 13 new body colors in conventional Two Tone and stunni[ng]
new Style Tone combinations.

Interior Styling: There are five all-vinyl, Luxury Lounge interiors availab[le]
Each features the special, new Airweave "breathable" vinyl in seat c[u]
hion and back inserts. Upholsteries and trims are color-keyed wi[th]
appropriate exterior body colors providing exquisite color harmony.

Engines: 212-hp Thunderbird 292 V-9—292 cu. in. displaceme[nt]
3.75" bore x 3.30" stroke; 9.1 to 1 compression ratio; regul[ar]
fuel. Low silhouette, 2-venturi carburetor. Single, Y-type exhau[st]
system.
245-hp Thunderbird 312 Special V-8 (opt.)—312 cu. in. displa[ce]
ment, 3.80" bore x 3.44" stroke; 9.7 to 1 compression rati[o]
premium fuel. Low-silhouette, 4-venturi carburetor. Dual exhau[st]
system.
300-hp Thunderbird 312 Supercharged V-8 (opt.)—312-cu. i[n.]
displacement; 3.80" bore x 3.44" stroke; 8.5 to 1 compressi[on]
ratio. Centrifugal-type supercharger with automatic ball-driv[e]
variable-speed blower control, engine-lubricated, dual V-be[lt]
drive. Sealed 4-venturi carburetor; premium fuel; du[al]
exhaust system. 18-gal. fuel tank has filler tube in le[ft]
rear fender.
All three engines are available with all transmissio[ns]

Clutch and Transmission: Semi-centrifugal clutch wi[th]
new full-weighted levers for more positive engagemen[t]
suspended pedal. Conventional Drive has 3 forwa[rd]
speeds and 1 reverse, with gear ratios tailored to eac[h]
engine. New shot-peened, finer-pitch helical gears f[or]
greater strength and quietness; forged bronze synch[ro]
nizers. Overdrive is combination of 3-speed transmissio[n]
plus an automatic 4th gear that cuts in at about 2[7]
mph, cuts out at about 22 mph.

Fordomatic Drive: Torque converter co[m]
bined with automatic gear mechanis[m]
Water-cooled. Three forward gears, 1 r[e]
verse. Automatic "low-gear" starts an[d]
"intermediate-gear" passing with select[or]
in Drive (DR) position. Illuminated s[e]
lector dial with steering-post-mounte[d]
lever for natural feel, natural sequenc[e]

Front Suspension: New, swept-back, Ball-Joint designs with one-piece stabilizer, Viscous-control shock absorbers.

Rear Suspension: New variable-rate type, full outboard mounted, long-leaved rear springs. Six leaves with friction-control inserts. Diagonally mounted Viscous-control shock absorbers.

Rear Axle: New, deep-offset hypoid, semi-floating type with exclusive straddle-mounted pinion.

Axle Ratios (to 1): Conventional Drive—3.89 standard, 4.11 optional; Overdrive—4.11 standard, Fordomatic Drive—3.56 standard.

Steering: Worm and triple-tooth gear mechanism. Anti-friction bearings throughout. Symmetrical linkage; 27 to 1 over-all ratio; 17½" dia., 3-spoke Lifeguard deep-dish steering wheel. Approx. 40" turning diameter. Master-Guide Power Steering optional at extra cost.

Brakes: Double-seal Giant-Grip hydraulic; suspended pedal; 11" drum; 191-sq. in. lining area. New, low-pedal type Swift Sure Power Brakes optional at extra cost.

Tires: Smaller, 8.00 x 14 tubeless; new 5½" safety-type rims. Spare tire stows flat on underside of trunk tire-well cover.

Wide-Contoured Frame: Specially designed, precision-made, 4-cross-member frame with I-beam X-member at center. Box-section side rails are widely flared to extend outside seating areas, afford passengers added protection, provide more foot room. Body-mounting brackets, welded to inner and outer sides of rails, help reduce road shock.

Dimensions: 118" wheelbase; 59.0" front, 56.4" rear treads. Over-all length, 210.8". Height (maximum with design load), 56.3".

Prices: All Power Assists and Accessories as well as some items illustrated or referred to herein are at extra cost. For the price of the Skyliner with the equipment you desire, see your Ford Dealer.

The specifications contained herein were in effect in April of 1957.

The new Ranchero, a convenient marriage of the passenger car luxury with the light duty truck rear cargo area was introduced in 1957. Built on a station wagon frame, and with some similarity to them, the Ranchero was successfully designed to provide a passenger-car comfortable cab and still offer a pick-up bed for cargo. Two models were offered, the Ranchero which was essentially a stripped-down version and the Custom Ranchero, a more popular car which included the side trim shown here as well as the expected subtle additional features including dual sun visors, horn rings, etc.

Shortened rear bumper guards are used to permit the tail gate to lie flat.

1957 Type 66 B Custom Ranchero Mr. Larry Evenson, Alamo, California

The Ranchero, like the station wagon body on which it is based, has a tailgate at the rear for loading and the fuel filler pipe is moved to the left side under an access cover.

Bright metal trim frames the rear window, and inside is a luxurious passenger car type interior.

A long steel bed, well suited to light weight hauling, is surrounded by a high-sided body for load security.

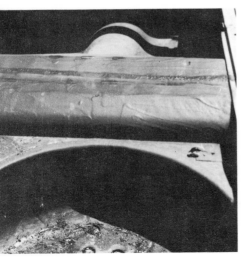

The spare wheel of the Ranchero is stored behind the seat in the passenger compartment, but by removing the steel floor, the customary station wagon type well is exposed along with the "floor" of the more conventional models.

* FAIRLANE SERIES

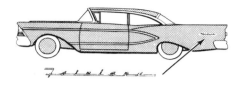

FAIRLANE

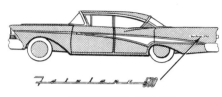

FAIRLANE "500"

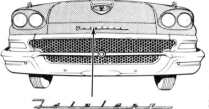

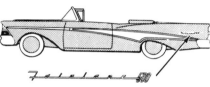

**FAIRLANE "500"
HIDE-AWAY HARDTOP**

FAIRLANE "500" CONVERTIBLE

* CUSTOM SERIES

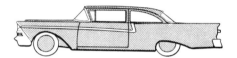

CUSTOM "300" - SPECIAL

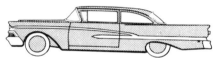

CUSTOM "300" STYLETONE

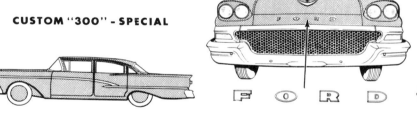

CUSTOM "300"

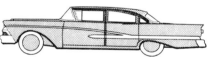

CUSTOM "300" STYLETONE

* STATION WAGONS, ETC.

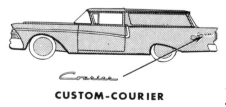

CUSTOM-COURIER

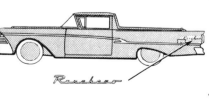

CUSTOM "300" RANCHERO

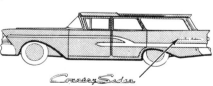

**CUSTOM "300" STYLETONE
COUNTRY SEDAN**

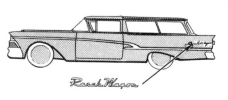

CUSTOM "300" RANCH WAGON

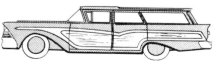

FAIRLANE "500" COUNTRY SQUIRE

*Does not include all body types.   Illustrations are representative models.

Route of the 1958 Round the World trip.

As a promotional gesture, an early 1958 Ford was driven around the world on a rugged torture test "using the entire earth as a test track". The car climbed the Alps, entered Paris, even crossed the great Salt Dert of Iran, and "zoomed up and through the Khyber Pass". It truly was a Tour to justify the headlines it received.

With much new in the styling, including a simulated air scoop on the hood, honeycomb grill (both reminiscent of the Thunderbird), and a sculptured rear deck treatment (also shared with the 1958 Thunderbird) plus the introduction of dual headlamps on each front fender, the styling is vastly advanced, far more startling than the 1957 cars. Although the custom line is dropped, the others are continued.

For 1958, a new transmission, the Cruise-O-Matic which offers smooth three-speed-range accelerations or alternate intermediate-and-high gear starts for gradual acceleration joins the earlier Ford-O-Matic and Overdrive as optional accessory transmissions. New body colors, and a choice of engines are offered including a 300 horsepower 352 cid Interceptor option on the Fairlane and Station Wagon series. The 1958 Fords offered an optional Ford-Aire suspension system, which maintained a constant car height under all load conditions, on the Fairlane 500, the Fairlane, and the Station Wagon Series. In this system, sturdy plastic "balloons" contained within the four coil springs (used on the rear in 1958 Air Suspensions only) are inflated to varying suitable pressures depending on the load. A built in, under the hood, air for the system while an automatic leveler compensates for variations in load and road conditions. Apparently troublesome, the Ford-Aire Suspension system was not again offered after 1958, but at the time there was "nothing newer in the World".

BODY STYLES

51 A Fairlane 500 Hi Skyliner
57 A Fairlane 500 Town Victoria
58 B Fairlane 500 Town Sedan
63 A Fairlane 500 Club Victoria
64 B Fairlane 500 Club Sedan
76 B. Fairlane 500 Convertible Coupe
57 B Fairlane Town Victoria
58 A Fairlane Town Sedan
63 B Fairlane Club Victoria
64 A Fairlane Club Sedan

70 A Custom 300 Tudor Sedan
70 B Same, optional trim package
70 D Custom 300 Business Tudor
73 A Custom 300 Fordor Sedan
73 B Same, optional trim package
59 A Tudor Ranch Wagon
59 B Tudor Ranch Wagon "Del Rio"
66 A Ranchero
66 B Custom Ranchero
79 A Fordor Ranch Wagon
79 D 6 Passenger Country Sedan
79 E 9 Passenger Country Squire

Exteriors and Interiors: A total of 13 exciting new body colors are available, all of gleaming, durable, baked-on enamel. All models come in Single Color or stunning new Style Tone, as well as Conventional Two Tone on Fairlane 500's. Interiors are beautifully upholstered with long-lasting leather-grained vinyl, woven plastic or nylon fabrics including exclusive new tweed pattern, in colors to harmonize with exteriors. See the complete selection at your Ford Dealer's.

Engines: *145-hp Mileage Maker Six*—223-cu. in. displ.; 3.62″ bore x 3.60″ stroke; 8.6 to 1 comp. ratio; regular fuel; manual choke. (For all models except Skyliner.)

205-hp Ford 292 V-8 (Optional on Fairlane and Custom 300)—292-cu. in. displ.; 3.75″ bore x 3.30″ stroke; 9.1 to 1 comp. ratio; regular fuel; low-silhouette 2-venturi carburetor, automatic choke.

New 240-hp Interceptor 332 V-8 (Optional on Station Wagons)—332-cu. in. displ.; 4.00″ bore x 3.30″ stroke; 9.5 to 1 comp. ratio; regular fuel; low-silhouette 2-venturi carburetor, automatic choke; self-adjusting hydraulic valve lifters.

New 265-hp Interceptor 332 Special V-8 (Optional all models)—332-cu. in. displ.; 4.00″ bore x 3.30″ stroke; 9.5 to 1 comp. ratio; regular fuel; low-silhouette 4-venturi carburetor, automatic choke; self-adjusting hydraulic valve lifters.

New 300-hp Interceptor 352 Special V-8 (Optional on Fairlane 500 and Station Wagons)—352-cu. in. displ.; 4.00″ bore x 3.50″ stroke; 10.2 to 1 comp. ratio; premium fuel; low-silhouette 4-venturi carburetor, automatic choke; self-adjusting hydraulic valve lifters.

Engine Features: For greater economy and longer life all engines have short-stroke, low-friction, deep-block design; free-turning overhead valves; Super-Filter air cleaner; full-pressure lubrication; Full-Flow oil filter; 12-volt electrical system; turbo-action 18-mm. spark plugs. V-8 engines are electronically balanced under own power for optimum smoothness. All Interceptor engines have Precision Fuel Induction for superior performance and economy.

Transmissions: *3-speed* with gear ratios tailored to each engine. Optional: *Overdrive* with automatic 4th gear. *Fordomatic Drive* with smooth-acting torque converter and three forward gears for normal or fast starting. *New Cruise-O-Matic* high performance automatic with two selective drive ranges for smooth 1-2-3 full-power getaway or 2-3 gradual acceleration and axle ratio of 2.69 to 1 for fuel economy (with Special V-8's only).

Suspension: Smoother-acting Angle-Poised, 4-way ball-joint front and variable-rate, outboard-mounted rear suspension.

Ford-Aire Suspension: Complete air cushion system for the utmost in smooth, soft riding, with automatic leveling valves to maintain constant car height, under all load conditions. (Optional on Fairlane, Fairlane 500 and Station Wagon models with Interceptor V-8's and automatic transmissions.)

Steering: New Magic-Circle recirculating-ball type for smoother, easier steering.

Other Available Equipment: Lifeguard padded instrument panel, cushioned sun visors, Ford seat belts. I-Rest tinted safety glass. SelectAire or PolarAire Conditioner, including tinted glass (V-8's only). Manually operated 4-way front seat. Heavy duty springs (for wagon models). Whitewall tires. Fuel-vacuum pump for positive-action windshield wipers.

1958 Type 51 A Fairlane 500 Skyliner

The Skyliner was continued into 1958 relatively unchanged. Basic changes included the trim stripes on the sides and similar items, but the most obvious change results from the use of dual headlights.

The 1958 Fairlane 500 bears a restyled stripe of distinctive design.

Mr. Rob Zarnosky, Granada Hills, California

The design of the trim at the roof quarter is unchanged from 1957 (page 246).

A simulated air scoop is introduced on the hood of the 1958 cars.

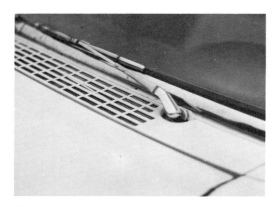

The incoming air for the passenger compartment ventilation is again placed just ahead of the windshield on the cowl.

Both Fairlane 500 and Fairlane series cars had this script name on the hood just above the grill. Custom 300 cars bear the name F-O-R-D.

A distinctive new gunsight fender ornament is placed above the Safety-Twin headlights. For high-beam driving, all four of these sealed beam lamps are illuminated.

Restyled parking lights are placed at the ends of the grill and protected by massive wrap-around bumpers.

The comfortable interior of the Skyliner exhibits excellent styling.

...ta plate appears on the left door pillar.

1958 uses same inside door handle as introduced in 1957 models.

Power-Lift windows, an optional extra cost accessory, are controlled from a central control panel on the driver's door, or by individual buttons at the windows.

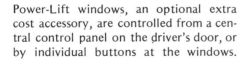

Although the general design and layout of the Skyliner rear end is typical of the 1958 model year, the need for added space in the luggage compartment in which to store the retracted top requires a somewhat more "square" deck appearance.

Dual tail lights combine the features of marker lights with brake-and-turn indicators as well. A new rectangular back-up light (optional equipment) is located between the tail lights.

The Fairlane script appears on the rear dec the 1958 model. There is no handle, but other models the lid is hinged at the front a keylock appears just above the script. leasing the lock permits the counterbalan hinges to raise the lid ofr access.

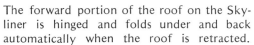

The forward portion of the roof on the Sky-liner is hinged and folds under and back automatically when the roof is retracted.

A stainless steel trim circles the windshield and the overhanging lip of the roof.

1958

1958 saw a continued excursion in the direction of higher horse-power engines although that characteristic itself was being soft-pedaled. Ford referred to its all-new 332 cubic inch engine as an "Interceptor 332 Special V-8" and offered the engine with a rating of 265 horse-power, about ten percent more than last year's Thunderbird Special 312.

The "big" engine for the year is the 352 cubic inch Interceptor Special V-8, a new 300 horsepower option rated at about the same as the 1957 **supercharged** 312. Available only with the Fairlane 500 models, this engine had a dress-up air cleaner readily identifying it when the hood was raised.

1958 Fairlane 500 Instrument panel.

A white knob appears on the transmission shift lever.

A matching white knob is placed on the turn signal lever.

As has become customary, when the Master Guide power steering option is selected, the horn ring bears its name.

To the right of the brake release handle suspended under the instrument panel is a knob to actuate the automatic mechanism which retracts and erects the top of the Skyliner and the Convertible coupe (Sunliner).

The position of the controls is unchanged from last year, but the trim plates change the appearance greatly.

n oil pressure warning light glows red below the fuel
vel gauge.

The Generator circuit charging light is placed at the right,
beneath the temperature gauge. The small lights at the
ends of the speedometer scale are turn signal indications.

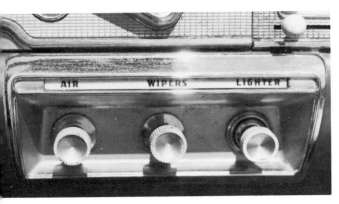

matching trim surrounds the customary controls to the right
f the speedometer.

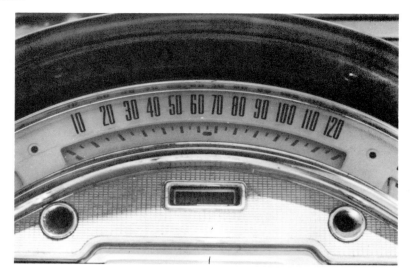

The instrument panel shrouds a semi-circular speedometer. Since 1955 speedometers have read 120 mph maximum.

The self-regulating electric clock is standard on the Fairlane 500 series and optional equipment on the others. Each time the clock is re-set, it automatically makes a rate correction in its speed.

The transistor-powered Console Range radio is push-button tuned to pre-set stations, but the volume control incorporates the OFF switch. The higher-priced Signal-Seek radio, which automatically tunes as well as incorporating the pre-set pushbuttons also has a push-button OFF switch.

The Fordomatic transmission position indicator is incorporated in the instrument panel at the base of the steering column.

A new insignia placed on the glove compartment door indicates that this automobile is equipped with the new 300 HP Interceptor Special 352 cid engine.

Station Wagons continued to be a big part of the Ford line in 1958, and Ford offered enough variations that one could almost design his own. There was the least expensive, the two door Ranch Wagon as illustrated on this page, there was a luxuriously trimmed version of the same car, similar to the 1957 Park Lane, wearing the Fairlane type stripe on its sides and called the "Del Rio", and the Country Squire, Ford's best-known station wagon. In addition, there were 6-and 9-passenger Country Sedans (all-metal bodies with Fairlane trim) and again, two versions of the Ranchero which had been introduced the previous year.

The Ranchero has the trim similar to that on the Ranch Wagon below, but the Custom Ranchero bears the Fairlane stripe as it appears on the other cars in that series as well as the usual dress-up items such as dual sun visors, horn rings, and chromed windshield mouldings.

1958 Type 59 A Ranch Wagon　　　　　　Mr. Rudy Vasquez, Poway, California

wheelcovers are incorrect style

The front end of the lower-priced Custom line lacks much of the trim of the Fairlane and Fairlane 500 series cars. As an example, there is no decorative "bullseye sight" on the fenders (page 256).

The Ford name appears on the hood in place of the Fairlane script.

The same front bumper is used on all lines. This massive unit wraps around the fender for maximum protection.

The grill of all lines bears the unique 1958 pattern.

Headlight visors on the Custom line cars do not have the chrome trim found on the Fairlanes (page 256).

Starting in 1957, the parking lamps are right-and left-handed pairs. Although different in style, the 1958 parking lights again are required in pairs.

The forward portion of the rear quarter windows slide to open. When closed, they are secured with a catch.

This is the basic Custom line trim for 1958. It appears on both Ranch Wagons, and unless the special trim package (Styletone) is ordered, the Tudor and Fordor Custom models.

The window pillar of the Ranch Wagon is painted, does not have trim. In the Del Rio model, a luxury-trimmed version of the same car, this area is decorated with a corrugated chromed trim plate.

Due to the need for a loading gate at the rear, the fuel filler pipe is moved to the left rear fender under an access flap.

he door sill of the Custom cars is simpler and less ttractive than the same area in the Fairlanes (page 59).

The chrome trim found over the windshield pillars of the Fairlane cars is missing on the Custom series.

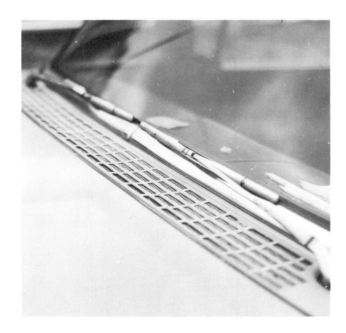

All cars in the 1958 Model year used these white-knobbed window cranks unless they were equipped with Power-Lift windows.

A wide tail gate lowers for access to the cargo compartment. This is the six passenger Ranch Wagon. There is no third seat.

Due to the need to split the tail lights for the installation of a tail gate, the back up lights on Station Wagons are round instead of rectangular (page 258). Interestingly, the 1958 Rancheros incorporate the typical 1957 rear end, and are the only models in the 1958 line to do so.

The High-Canted rear fenders of the 1957 line are continued, although modified, on the 1958 cars.

The roof overhangs the chrome-trimmed rear window.

The second seat is secured by a catch at the right side. Releasing this enables the seat back to be rotated forward for added cargo space.

The cargo deck of the rear compartment hides the spare wheel storage area which is reached through a hinged plate in the floor (below).

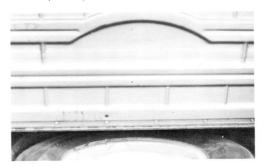

An accessory inside non-glare mirror became available in 1958.

There is no horn ring (and only one inside sun visor) furnished with the low-priced Ranch Wagon.

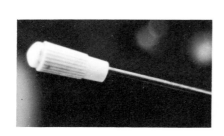

Only black steering wheels are used in the economy line of cars.

The horn button bears the name Ford, but not the crest.

The speedometer cluster is nicely framed in the three-spoke steering wheel.

The economy hot water heater is installed in this car. Control for this inexpensive heater-defroster is a single knob placed on the instrument panel just to the right of the speedometer in the area that would have contained the control head for the Magic Aire system.

"The World's Most Beautifully Proportioned Cars"

✱ FAIRLANE SERIES

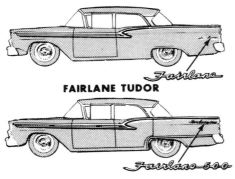

FAIRLANE TUDOR

FAIRLANE "500" FORDOR

FAIRLANE "500" HIDE-AWAY HARDTOP—SKYLINER

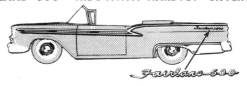

FAIRLANE "500" CONVERTIBLE—SUNLINER

✱ CUSTOM "300" SERIES

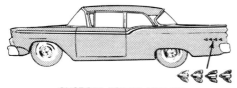

CUSTOM "300" TUDOR

CUSTOM "300" FORDOR

✱ STATION WAGONS, ETC.

**TUDOR CUSTOM "300"
RANCH WAGON**

**CUSTOM "300"
RANCHERO**

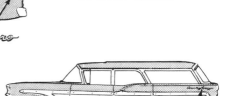

**FAIRLANE "500"
FORDOR RANCH WAGON
COUNTRY SEDAN**

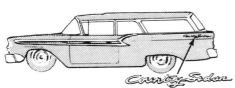

**FAIRLANE "500"
TUDOR RANCH WAGON—COUNTRY SEDAN**

**FAIRLANE "500"
COUNTRY SQUIRE**

✱ Does not include all body types.   Illustrations are representative models

Considered by many to be the most beautifully styled Fords ever built, the 1959 Ford was awarded a Gold Medal for Exceptional Styling at the Brussels World Fair. With a great elegance and under-stated **class** the car bore unmistakable lines of good taste and restraint. In an era where tail "fins" were all the rage with other manufacturers, Ford had merely swept the rear fender lines straight to the back of the car, formed a housing for the back-up lights at the top, and curved the lower portion around an over-size taillight for remarkable effect. At the front end, the fenders were flatted across the top to house the dual headlights, and had an added sculptured effect at the sides where they rolled over the side trim. Long, low, with exceptionally flat hood and deck cover, the car bore relatively little in the way of adornment and depended for best effect on startling colors and combinations of color.

A new 350 HP, 352 CID engine was an optional offering, and a new, wider, front grill extended from side to side (parking lights were recessed into the bumper), and late in 1958 a whole new series called the Galaxie was introduced which employed the same quarter window and rear quarter styling as the Thunderbird making this one of the best recognized cars on the road on the day it was introduced.

The Custom (not the Custom 300) line was dropped in 1959 and after the introduction of the Galaxie, early in the year, demand for the Fairlane Series was reduced. The highly sculptured lines of the 1959 series persisted though and the cars basked in the glory of the award earned as "the world's most beautifully proportioned cars".

BODY TYPES

51 A	Galaxie Skyliner		58 C	Fairlane Town Sedan
54 A	Galaxie Town Sedan		64 A	Fairlane Club Sedan
64 H	Galaxie Club Sedan		58 C	Custom 300 Fordor Sedan
65 A	Galaxie Club Victoria		64 F	Custom 300 Tudor Sedan
75 A	Galaxie Town Victoria		64 G	Custom 300 Business Tudor
76 B	Galaxie Convertible Coupe (Sunliner)		59 D	2-door Ranch Wagon
57A	Fairlane 500 Town Victoria		71 H	4-door Ranch Wagon
58 B	Fairlane 500 Town Sedan		71 E	9-passenger Country Sedan
67 A	Fairlane 500 Club Victoria		71 F	6-passenger Country Sedan
64 B	Fairlane 500 Club Sedan		71 G	Country Squire
			66 A	Ranchero
			66 C	Custom Ranchero

Exteriors: Amazing new Diamond Lustre Finish, most durable body finish ever developed, is available in Single Color, Conventional Two Tone or Style Tone selections.

Basic colors are: Raven Black, Gunsmoke Gray, Colonial White, Surf Blue, Wedgewood Blue, Sherwood Green, April Green, Tahitian Bronze, Fawn Tan and Torch Red for all series, plus Inca Gold for Fairlanes and Inca Gold, Geranium and Indian Turquoise for Fairlane 500's.

Interiors: This year Ford introduces long-wearing nylon fabrics in all car series. Another Ford "first" is the use of an all-new Radiant Sof-Textured vinyl trim. This new vinyl has a super-high-metallic coating that gives the interior a brighter, more spacious effect. Floor covering in Custom 300 models is Sof-Tred carpet-textured black rubber. Fairlane models have color-keyed Vinyl-Tex, which looks like carpeting, wears like vinyl. Fairlane 500 models have color-coordinated deep-loop Luxury-Loom carpets.

See the complete selection of colors and fabrics at your Ford Dealer's.

Engines: 145-hp Mileage Maker Six—223-cu. in. displ.; 3.62" bore x 3.60" stroke, 8.4 to 1 comp. ratio; regular fuel; manual choke.

200-hp Thunderbird 292 V-8 (Standard V-8 on all models)—292-cu. in. displ.; 3.75" bore x 3.30" stroke, 8.8 to 1 comp. ratio; regular fuel; low-silhouette 2-venturi carburetor, automatic choke, Y-type single exhaust.

225-hp Thunderbird 332 Special V-8 (Optional on all models)—332-cu. in. displ.; 4.00" bore x 3.30" stroke, 8.9 to 1 comp. ratio; premium fuel; low-silhouette 2-venturi carburetor, automatic choke, Y-type single exhaust.

300-hp Thunderbird 352 Special V-8 (Optional on all models)—352-cu. in. displ.; 4.00" bore x 3.50" stroke, 9.6 to 1 comp. ratio; premium fuel; low-silhouette 4-venturi carburetor, automatic choke, dual exhausts.

Engine Features: For greater economy and longer life, all Ford engines have Short Stroke, low-friction design, with Deep-Block construction; intake and exhaust valves of free-turning, overhead type; Super-Filter air cleaner with reusable paper element; vacuum-booster fuel pump for more constant windshield-wiper action; full-pressure lubrication with Full-Flow disposable-type oil filter; weatherproof, high-capacity 12-volt electrical system; Turbo-Action 18-mm. spark plugs designed for increased gas mileage; exhaust system featuring new aluminized muffler. V-8 engines are electronically balanced while operating under their own power for extra smoothness. Thunderbird Special V-8's feature self-adjusting, hydraulic valve lifters for quietness and Precision Fuel Induction for superior performance and economy.

Fordomatic Drive: All new for '59, Fordomatic uses a single-stage, 3-element torque converter and a compound planetary gear set. These are incorporated into an automatic mechanism that requires only one clutch assembly to provide two "forward" gear ratios . . . low and direct . . . and reverse. In "D" range it provides brisk, smooth starts in low. This simplified design uses 27% fewer parts and with its cast-aluminum construction is much lighter in weight. This new Fordomatic is so dependable that after initial 1000-mile band adjustment, it requires normal servicing only each 24,000 miles. Available with all engines.

Cruise-O-Matic Drive: A high performance automatic featuring two selective drive ranges—smooth 3-speed operation in "D₁" range, starting in low for solid, full-power getaways and all normal driving . . . or 2-speed operation in "D₂" range,

starting in intermediate for gentle, sure-footed acceleration on ice, snow or loose gravel. Coupled with specially tailored gas-saving rear axle ratios, it provides "built-in" overdrive economy. Available with all V-8 engines.

Wide-Contoured Frame: Strong, stiff, box-section frame with 5 cross members. Side rails extend outside passenger area, for better foot room and increased side protection. Silent-Grip body mounting system.

Suspension: Swept-Back, Angle-Poised Ball-Joint front suspension has threaded, permanently lubricated bushings in upper control arms for soft, easy ride. Front end of all models has new link-type, rubber-bushed ride stabilizer to control roll on turns. Even-Keel rear springs provide soft action, variable rate with tension-type shackles and wind-up control rubber bumpers over springs. Viscous-control shock absorbers front and rear, give complete ride control.

Rear Axle: Husky, low-slung hypoid, semi-floating with special Deep-Offset straddle-mounted pinion, permits lower car level without sacrifice of inside room.

Torque-Tailored Axle Ratios (to 1): Conventional Drive—3.56 (std.) or 3.70 (opt.) with Six; 3.56 with 292 V-8 or 352 Special V-8. Overdrive—3.70 with Six or 292 V-8, 3.56 with 352 Special V-8. Fordomatic Drive—3.56 with Six, 3.10 with 292 V-8, 2.91 with 332 or 352 Special V-8's. Cruise-O-Matic Drive—3.10 with 292 V-8, 2.91 with 332 Special V-8, 2.69 with 352 Special V-8.

Optional Equa-Lock Differential Ratios (to 1): 3.70 with Six, 292 V-8 or 352 Special V-8 and 3-speed or Overdrive; also Six and Fordomatic—3.10 with 292 V-8, 332 or 352 Special V-8's and Fordomatic or Cruise-O-Matic.

STEERING: Magic-Circle recirculating-ball type steering gear provides low friction, easy steering. 27 to 1 over-all steering ratio. 17½", 3-spoke, deep-center Lifeguard steering wheel. Approximately 40-foot turning diameter.

BRAKES: Giant-Grip double-sealed, self-energizing hydraulic brakes have suspended pedal, dash-mounted master cylinder. Drum diameter is 11". Lining area is 180 sq. in. Optional Swift Sure power brakes have special low pedal and power reserve tank.

Tires: 7.50 x 14 inch, 4-ply black tubeless tires of new Tyrex super cord on 5" safety-type rims.

Dimensions: 118" wheelbase on all models; 59.0" front, 56.4" rear treads. Over-all length, 208.0". Height (maximum with design load) 56.0". For other dimensions, see illustration at left.

Other Available Equipment: Power front seat, Swift Sure power brakes, Master-Guide power steering, Power-Lift windows (except Business Sedan), Overdrive, Fordomatic Drive, Cruise-O-Matic Drive. White sidewall tires.

275

With top up, the Skyliner is comparable to the Club Victoria.

1959 Type 51 A Galaxie Hide-Away Hardtop (Skyliner)

With top down, the Skyliner is comparable to the Convertible Coupe.

Mr. Stanley Clapper, Clinton, Wisconsin

Side reflector strips have been added, are not factory installed.

1959

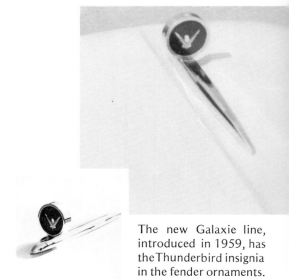

The new Galaxie line, introduced in 1959, has the Thunderbird insignia in the fender ornaments.

Fairlane 500, Fairlanes, and Country Sedans have a ball-shaped fender ornament.

A new rendition of the familiar Ford crest appears on the Galaxie line of cars.

An embossed channel runs along the top of the fenders adding to the appearance.

The highly sculptured, overhanging lip of the fenders is trimmed with bright metal on the Galaxie line.

Parking lights are placed in the fenders, and being round, are no longer required in pairs.

*All 1959 cars are built on the 118"
wheelbase chassis, with an over-all
length of 208" (Skyliner is 211.0)
about 1 inch longer than the 1958
models.*

A view through the windshield shows the
double-swivel rear view mirror.

The antenna has an oval base, and
still bears the distinctive crimped ring
at the foot of its mast.

A reconfigured front door assembly (page 259)
finds the windshield post sweeping still further
back to a sharp corner at its base, and gaining
a curve at its top into which the vent window
assembly fits.

The wide rear window is framed by a unique trim piece giving
the impression of a ventilation exhaust.

1959

The sculptured lines of the 1959 Ford are apparent in the overhang of the front fender and the curves of the rear.

As a part of the over-all restyling of 1959, outside door handles are placed over a recess in the door panels.

The Skyliner door panel is elaborate and distinctive.

Inside handles are unchanged from 1958.

The data plate is continued on the left door post.

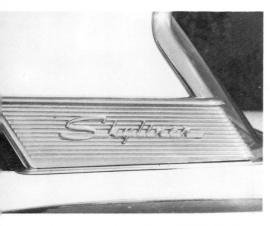

The roof quarter trim of the 1959 Skyliner bears its name, but unlike 1957-58, it no longer has the Ford Crest included (page 255).

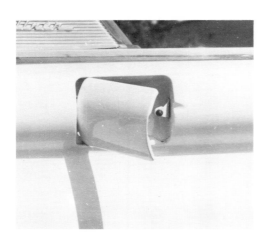

The fuel filler tube of the Skyliner is reached through an access door far forward on the left rear fender. Aside from station wagons, other models continued to offer center-fill fueling behind the license plate holder.

The dress-up bright metal trim behind the wheel well is standard on the Galaxies and Fairlane 500, but does not appear on the Fairlane and Custom series cars.

New in 1959 is the Galaxie series, initially a part of the Fairlane 500, but later to supercede it. For a time, both Fairlane 500 and Galaxie/Fairlane 500 models were built. This is the Galaxie script appearing on the rear fender of such cars.

The Fairlane 500 insignia and the wide-spread chrome trim appears on the rear of that series and also of the Galaxie versions such as the Skyliner.

The massive bumper dips to accommodate the large round tail lights.

Larger, round tail lights in 1959 combine Turn, Stop, and Marker functions into one beautifully styled package.

Back up lights are standard on the Fairlane 500 and Galaxie starting in 1959 and are placed in standard lamps nicely fitted into the back of the fender. At extra cost, bulbs and wiring are added on other models.

The control for the Sky-liner's retractible top is chromed.

The three-spoked deep-center steering wheel first used in 1956 is continued into 1959. In the Galaxie models, these were dressed up by including a contrasting color on the spokes.

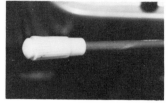

Turn signals are standard. The knob matches the shift lever knob.

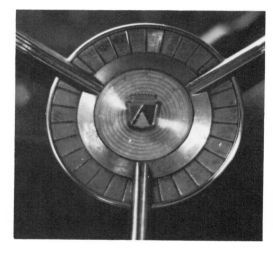

The horn ring bears the words "Power Steering" (right) if that option has been selected.

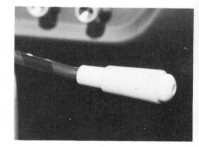

Transmission shift lever is unchanged.

A foot-operated parking brake appears in 1959.

The hood release knob is suspended beneath the instrument panel.

An excellent view of the instrument panel is obtained through the three-spoked steering wheel.

Above the Fuel level gauge is an arrow illuminated as the left turn signal. To its lower right is the OIL pressure warning light.

The generator Charge warning light and the Right turn signal indication are placed to the right of the speedometer.

Knobs, positions, and functions are unchanged from 1958, but the styling of the area has been changed with good effect.

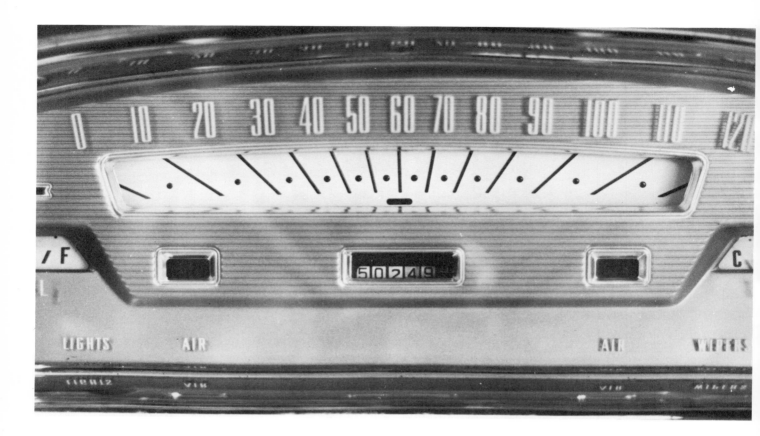

A new transmission, Cruise-O-Matic, had been introduced in 1958. With all of the features of the earlier Fordomatic transmissions, it added an extra D1 position which enabled "jackrabbit" starts from low gear or intermediate-gear starts in the D2 position. The indicator for either automatic transmission remains on the instrument panel. This is the Cruise-O-Matic transmission indicator which includes the D1 and D2 positions. Compare with a Fordomatic scale on page 264.

Directly beneath the radio at the center of the 1959 instrument panel the "bin" type ash tray (first introduced in 1957). Suspended beneath it is a courtesy light in the Skyliner, this light replaces the dome or pillar lights of the closed cars.

The control head for the optional Magic Aire heating and ventilating system is built into the instrument panel to the right of the speedometer. The built-in factory accessory Select Aire conditioner utilizes a similar control head incorporating the air conditioning function which replaces this control head.

1959

The Signal Seek radio, also transistor-powered, adds automatic station tuning.

Again two radios are offered. This is the Console Range lower-priced model.

The self-regulating electric clock, standard on Fairlane 500 and Galaxie models is an optional extra cost accessory on the others.

Both the Fairlane 500 *and* the Galaxie names appear on the glove box door. A new pushbutton lock is set into the lid

1959 Type 54A Galaxie Town Sedan

1959 Type 75 A Galaxie Town Victoria

Galaxie models have the Thunderbird fender ornament.

The roof slightly overhangs the wide rear window glass and chromed trim lines the area.

With the windows retracted the Town Victoria has no center post.

The Adjust-O-Ring mirror is an accessory.

The 1959 rear fender has an obvious over-hang at the top. Galaxie models have the script name at the back of the fenders.

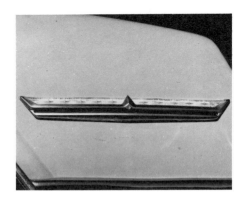

Close examination of the roof quarter trim discloses a resemblence to the Ford crest.

The 1959 Galaxie Town Sedan has a roof quarter greatly reminiscent of the Thunderbird. Although its slender trim retracts with the window, the pillar between the front and rear windows does not.

The 1959 Galaxie Town Victoria has an interesting trim piece added on the rear door which entirely changes the appearance of the area. This section opens with the door (right).

Station wagons were at the height of their popularity by 1959. Ford offered five different models from the two-door Ranch Wagon to the top-of-the-line Country Sedan. There was a model for every purpose and this nine passenger Type 71 E Country Sedan was a popular choice. This picture, taken in 1959 by Glenn Embree as a suggested illustration for a Ford ad, typifies the high interest that then existed in such vehicles. For the outdoorsman, there was nothing more to be desired than a Ford "wagon" and accompanying house trailer. Later, the advent of the "mobile home" self-contained home-on-wheels and the inbetween "vans" would cause a decline in the popularity of rigs such as the one shown here, but in 1959, this is the way that it was.

1959 Type 66 C Custom Ranchero

Mr. William Macauley, San Diego, California

A full-width tail gate is styled smartly between the distinctive 1959 tail lights.

A large cargo area extends from the back of the cab to the tailgate interrupted only by the wheel housings.

The bright metal trim on the headlight visors (page 278) is omitted on the Ranchero.

The name F-O-R-D appears on the front of the hood in place of the Crest of the Galaxie and Fairlane 500 cars.

The Ranchero script appears on the rear fenders.

The rear window of the Ranchero has a distinctive trim which flows back along the sides of the cargo bed.

The wide rear window is flat, unlike the curved glass in other models.

The unique insignia on the tail gate is that of the Ranchero and is not used elsewhere.

WHEEL COVERS & HUB CAPS

1942

Wheels were striped until 1949, not afterwards.

1946

1947-48

1949

The former 16" wheels were joined by an optional 15" wheel available starting in 1949.

1950

1950 dress up wheel cover

15" wheels became standard on the Custom Deluxe and optional on the Deluxe.

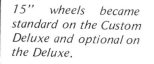

1950 Crestliner

1951

1951 Crestliner

In each year of manufacture, Ford furnished a "standard" hub cap which could be optionally dressed up initially with beauty rings, later with wheel covers which concealed almost the entire wheel. After about the mid-fifties, virtually all cars were furnished with the "dress-up" covers at the customer's expense.

*15" wheels became standard on
all cars in 1953.*

1952 accessory full wheel
cover and standard hub
cap (right).

1953 hub cap (right) and accessory wheel cover (above).

1954 hub cap

1954 accessory wheel cover

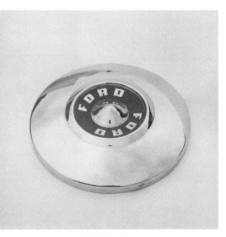

1955 hub cap

1955 accessory wheel cover —
*also available is the accessory wire
wheel cover (see next page)*

1956 hub cap

1955-56 Accessory wire wheel cover. This cover fits *over* the standard hub cap and is shown here installed over a 1956 hub cap (left).

1956 accessory wheel cover

14" wheels became standard on all models in 1957.

1957 hub cap

1957 accessory wheel cover

1958 accessory wheel cover

1959 wheel cover. This year, for the first time, there is no small hub cap available.

1959 Sun Ray dress up centers for the 1959 wheel cover

PROMOTIONAL MODELS

Shortly after World War II, the Ford Motor Company commenced the practice of distributing what are called "Miniatures" of the current car as a promotional effort. These miniatures, approximately seven or eight inches in overall length are understandably of varying degrees of faithfulness of representation, and as might be expected, the latest ones are most closely accurate in their nature.

The Collection of these miniatures, and also the popular assembly kit models, is a hobby unto itself, and we are indebted to Mr. Larry Blodgett, President of The Fabulous Fifties Ford Club of America for opening his splendid collection to our cameras and to him additionally for the identifications.

1947-48 Sedan
Pot metal die casting
by Master-Caster, Chicago, Illinois

Later model 1949 Fordor on left has flaws (above) corrected. AMT.

Early model of 1949 Fordor, note no trunk handle, no name on hood, reversed rear door handles. Made by AMT of Tenite, the first year this plastic was used for this purpose. (AMT had also built an aluminum 1948 model.)

(from left)
- 1950 metal bank has bumper guards, by Banthrico, Inc.
- 1950 AMT Tenite with wind-up motor, no bumper guards, no vent windows (also shown at right)
- Re-issued (1962) AMT 1950 Convertible kit

1950 Fordor sedan, AMT

1951 Fordor sedan. Has V-8 on front fender just above the Customline insignia. Aluminum chassis was introduced this year. AMT

1952 Customline Fordor. First year to have the plastic windows and friction motors in Ford miniatures.

1953 Fordor

1953 Sunliner, (AMT's first Convertible Ford), and 1953 Customline Fordor with Coronado Deck kit. In addition, there is a rare commemorative 1953 Indianapolis Pace Car model complete with decals.

1953 was the first year for an interior representation on *any* AMT plastic model.

PROMOTIONAL MODELS

1954 Customline Fordor. This is the first two-toning of plastic models; also the first to have non-plastic (jeweled) tail lights.

1954 Sunliner; interior is greatly improved over the 1953 model.

1955 Victoria; "chromed" wheel covers. (also shown below right) and die cast 1955 Sunliner with chromed grill.

1955 Tudor Sedan

1956 Victoria, two-toned paint and white wall tires.

1957 Victoria

1957
(clockwise from the top)
— Country Squire
— Skyliner
— Victoria
— Custom 300 Tudor
— Ranch Wagon

1958 Fairlane 500 Club Victoria

1958 Fairlane 500 Club Victoria with 1958 Sunliner.

1959
— Fairlane 500 Club Victoria
— Galaxie Club Victoria
  note difference in roof quarters

PROMOTIONAL MODELS

1959 Galaxie Skyliner

1959 Fairlane 500 Club Victoria

1959, seven models
(clockwise from the top)
— Country Sedan
— Ranchero
— Fairlane 500 Convertible
— Galaxie Convertible
— Galaxie Club Victoria
— Skyliner
— Fairlane 500 Club Victoria

1955-56-57-58-59 Station Wagons
by Product Miniature Co. (PMC)
(1955 and 56 only had vents in rear door windows)

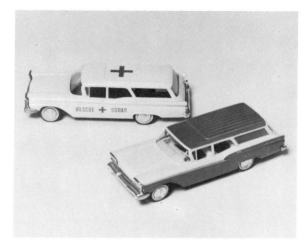

1959 Ambulance
1959 6-passenger Country Sedan

1953 50th Anniversary model
— Banthico polished metal model

An interesting 1955 Ford Tractor

1953 Victoria, plastic bank

1952 Meteor, a Canadian Ford

1958 Skyliner, a Japanese metal model

Revel 1/32 scale plastic kits:
1957 Country Squire   1959 Skyliner
1955 Sunliner   1956 Sunliner

PROMOTIONAL MODELS

During this period, the breakfast cereal producers issued premiums with their products, and among these were small (about 2") one-piece plastic Fords. Of various colors, shapes, and models, they are not here cataloged.

POST cereals . were popular and many different models were distributed with their breakfast foods.

Kellogg's also distributed similar, but not identical, premiums.

Grill guards were a popular accessory during this period. Models were available for the front, for the rear, and there were even some "wings" to extend the protection to the corners of the car.

1946

1949

1951 rear guard

1956 rear "wings"

1957

1959 Cushion-Stop bumper guards (front and rear) are rubber-tipped.

SOME ACCESSORIES

Back-up lights are a popular item which remained an accessory throughout the period until standardized on the 1959 Fairlane 500 series. All operate through a switch on the transmission linkage.

1946-48

1949-51

1952-54

1955 (see page 208 for 1956)

1957

1958

1959

1947

Rear view mirrors are now a requirement, but during the period they were always an accessory. Mirrors were offered as factory items, but more often were added by Dealers with conflicing results. Shown are "typical" styles as offered by the factory.

1950

1953

1953-56 style had no hole at the forward end; was mounted with a screw from underneath.

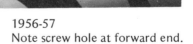

1956-57
Note screw hole at forward end.

1957

1957-58

1958-59

309

SOME ACCESSORIES

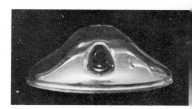

"Cobra head" jeweled exhaust deflector

1949-51

Fender Shields, as they were called by the factory, were frequently used to dress up the car. Adding but little to the appearance, they were frequently discarded at the first tire change.

1952-54

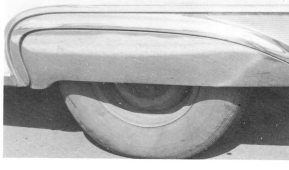

1955-56

1959

The 1949-51 windshield washer accessory bottle was replaced in 1952 with the See-Clear vinyl bag. The nozzle (right) on the hood appeared in 1952.

1951 locking gas door and trim

1949 accessory trim

Factory-installed air conditioning was first reported by Motor magazine to be available in the 1955 Ford. By 1956, the Ford catalogs showed a built-in unit suspended behind the instrument panel with vents exiting around the radio speaker grill. Replaced in 1957 with a unit exiting at the foot of the windshield, air conditioning has been a popular factory-installed option ever since.

An identification plate is placed on the door of the air conditioned 1957 model.

The 1957 factory-installed air conditioner, built behind the instrument panel, has cooling air at the base of the windshield.

Control unit for the air conditioner replaces the MagicAire head and now includes the cooling function.

Ford crest appears in center of vent.

1959 Select Aire Conditioner is behind instrument panel and includes appropriate ducts for combined heating, cooling, and ventilating. Only its chromed output assembly appears beneath the instrument panel. This unit was offered with the V-8 engine only. Alternately, a smaller Polar Aire unit was bolted on beneath the panel.

SOME ACCESSORIES

The *Coronado Deck* is an interesting accessory offered by Ford in 1953. It is a heavy gauge sheet metal assembly designed to be bolted onto the luggage compartment for added beauty. No alterations other than relocating the Fordomatic or Overdrive nameplates are necessary.

Access to the luggage compartment lock is made through a spring-loaded stainless steel "wheel cover" at the center. The license plate frame and wheel cover are stainless steel, the balance is painted to match the car.

1957 Continental kit with dress-up Fairlane trim (original is Ford crest)

1959 Continental kit

Continental kits include a rear deck and brackets to extend the bumper rearward. This 1959 model shows matching pattern for tail light lens.

"Continental" rear-mounted spare wheel kits are another factory accessory that has become extremely rare. Desired for their sporty appearance as well as the increased luggage space obtained by removing the spare to the rear, they reflect the 1956 Thunderbird styling on which they were standard and thus are not infrequently seen on passenger cars of the era.

1946 100 horsepower Ford V-8
- "flathead" style
- "pancake" distributor
- breather at rear oil filler tube
- color: gray

As a guide to those interested in identifying their engines from obvious distinguishing characteristics, we present an over-all view of the engines employed during this period and their significant outward features.

1946 90 Horsepower Ford SIX
- 4-blade fan
- exhaust on right side
- "pancake" distributor
- oil filter on left
- color: green with black accessories

1953 110 Horsepower High Compression Strato-Star V-8
- 3-blade fan
- new distributor
- "flathead" style
- breather at left front oil filler tube front-mounted cross-over pipe color: red with black accessories

1953 101 Horsepower High Compression Mileage Maker SIX
- 3-blade fan
- Distributor at right center
- oil filter on right side
- breather at oil filler tube at front
- fuel pump forward right side
- color: red with black accessories and silver valve cover

1954 130 Horsepower Y-Block V-8
  – overhead valves and valve covers
  – exhaust cross-over at top front
  – re-located fuel pump
  – breather at oil filler tube, top right
  – distributor at the rear
  – generator at lower right side

115 Horsepower I-Block Mileage Maker SIX
  – distributor at front right
  – fuel pump near right center

1954 engine blocks were painted ivory with black accessories and red valve covers and oil bath air cleaner.

1955-57 engines are red with black accessories and grey air cleaners.

1956 202 Horsepower Thunderbird Y-8
  – four-barrel carburator
  – dual exhausts
  – 4-blade fan
  – "Thunderbird" decal on valve covers

1959 300 Horsepower Thunderbird 352 Special V-8
— engine and accessories blue with blue valve covers and air cleaner

Also available:
  225 Horsepower Thunderbird 332 Special V-8
  — engine and accessories blue with green valve covers and air cleaner
  200 Horsepower Thunderbird 292 V-8
  — engine and accessories blue with red valve covers and accessories
  145 Horsepower Mileage Maker SIX
  — engine and accessories blue with red valve cover and air cleaner

1956

1957

ENGINES

1956

1953

The name "Interceptor" was applied in 1958 to the 300 HP 352 Thunderbird Special engine. Its air cleaner carried special decals and the glove box door was decorated with this Thunderbird Special nameplate.

During the period, Ford had four transmission options. A three-speed sliding gear manual transmission was standard. At extra cost, Ford offered OVERDRIVE, a two-speed automatic-shifting gear box placed in the drive line just behind the standard transmission. At approximately 25 miles per hour, the unit automatically shifted to reduce the engine-to-rear-end ratio. Principal advantage of the Overdrive is to reduce engine rpm and fuel consumption. 24-25 miles per gallon with Overdrive is not unusual against 18-20 for standard transmission.

Ford's first automatic transmission, FORDOMATIC, was introduced in 1951 and is significant for the fact that its shift pattern (P-R-N-D-L) has become the international standard shift sequence on automatic transmissions while other automatics of the period having different shift patterns have been discontinued. The early Fordomatic was a two-stage automatic-shifting transmission starting in INTERMEDIATE (2nd) gear and shifting to HIGH. Later versions, had a quicker start obtained by adding a capability of LOW-INTERMEDIATE-HIGH sequence on demand.

Ford's CRUISE-O-MATIC offered automatic transmission with three-stage shifting OR an alternate position in which LOW gear was locked out, almost a return the initial Fordomatic units. Jack rabbit starts and rear wheel spins are almost unheard of in this mode, yet smooth acceleration from start to HIGH is obtained.

V-8

Year	Data Plate Designation	Cubic Inch Displacement	Compression	Bore & Stroke	Horsepower	Carburetor
1946	—	239.4	6.15:1	3.187x3.75	100	2V
1947	—	239.4	6.8:1	3.187x3.75	100	2V
1948	—	239.4	6.75:1	3.187x3.75	100	2V
1949	—	239.4	6.8:1	3.187x3.75	100	2V
1950	—	239	6.8:1	3.187x3.75	100	2V
1951	—	239	6.8:1	3.187x3.75	100	2V
1952-1953	P	239	6.8:1	3.18x3.75	106	2V
1954	U	239	7.2:1	3.50x3.10	130	2V
1954	P	256	7.2:1	3.62x3.10	161	4V
1955	U	272	7.6:1	3.62x3.30	162	2V
1955	M	272	8.5:1	3.62x3.30	182	4V
1955	P	292	7.6:1	3.75x3.30	198	4V
1956	U	272	8.4:1	3.62x3.30	176	2V
1956	M	292	8.4:1	3.75x3.30	202	4V
1956	P	312	9.0:1	3.80x3.44	225	
1957	B	272	8.6:1	3.62x3.30	190	2V
1957	C	292	9.1:1	3.75x3.30	212	2V
1957	D	312	9.7:1	3.80x3.44	245	4V
1957	E	312	9.7:1	3.80x3.44	270	two 4V
1957	F	312	9.7:1	3.80x3.44	300	Supercharged
1958	C	292	9.1:1	3.75x3.30	205	2V
1958	B	332	9.5:1	4.00x3.30	240	2V
1958	G	332	9.5:1	4.00x3.30	265	4V
1958	H	352	10.2:1	4.00x3.50	300	4V
1959	C	292	8.8:1	3.75x3.30	200	2V
1959	B	332	8.9:1	4.00x3.30	225	2V
1959	H	332	9.6:1	4.00x3.50	300	4V
1959	H	430	10.0:1	4.30x3.70	350	4V

SIX

Data Plate Designation	Cubic Inch Displacement	Compression	Bore & Stroke	Horsepower
—	225.9	6.7:1	3.3x4.4	90
—	225.9	6.8:1	3.3x4.4	95
—	225.9	6.8:1	3.3x4.4	95
—	225.9	6.8:1	3.3x4.4	95
—	225.9	6.8:1	3.3x4.4	95
—	225.9	6.8:1	3.3x4.4	95
A	215	7.0:1	3.56x3.60	101
A	223	7.2:1	3.62x3.60	115
A	223	7.5:1	3.62x3.60	120
A	223	8.0:1	3.62x3.60	132
A	223	8.6:1	3.62x3.60	144
A	223	8.6:1	3.62x3.60	145
A	223	8.4:1	3.62x3.60	145

PRODUCTION FIGURES

PRODUCTION BY TYPE FOR THE TWELVE MONTHS ENDING DECEMBER 31st

1948
Ford

	SIX	V-8	
70 A Tudor	7,313	37,255	
72 A Club Coupe	469	3,701	
72 C Business Coupe	2,473	7,095	
73 A Fordor	2,926	7,386	
Totals	*13,181*	*55,437*	
Total Fords			*68,618*

Ford Custom

70 B Tudor	31,410	178,158	
72 B Club Coupe	10,970	82,831	
73 B Fordor	16,183	123,502	
76 Convertible Coupe	101	21,954	
79 Station Wagon	139	15,207	
Totals	*58,805*	*421,654*	*480,459*
Total Passenger Cars			*549,077*

1949
Deluxe

70 A Tudor	34,969	83,315	
72 A Club Coupe			
72 C Business Coupe	8,758	16,677	
73 A Fordor	12,121	29,054	
Total Deluxe	*55,849*	*129,046*	

Custom Deluxe

70 B Tudor	54,438	272,697	
72 B Club Coupe	11,789	77,468	
73 B Fordor	18,887	158,721	
76 Convertible Coupe	—	39,984	
79 Station Wagon	9	22,264	
Total Custom Deluxe	*85,126*	*571,149*	
Total Passenger Cars			*841,170*

1950
Deluxe

70 A Tudor	121,396	145,036	
72 C Business Coupe	17,646	15,831	
73 A Fordor	30,222	46,489	
Total Deluxe	*169,264*	*207,356*	

Custom

60 Victoria	—	4	
70 B Tudor	73,716	311,428	
72 B Club Coupe	11,933	69,309	
70 C Crestline	—	19,446	
73 B Fordor	28,915	222,748	
76 Convertible Coupe	—	49,399	
79 B Station Wagon	1,072	22,486	
Total Custom	*115,636*	*694,820*	
Total Passenger Cars			*1,187,076*

Figures from the Ford Motor Company Production records as extracted and compiled by the Author. Reflecting certain compensatory entries made in the original tabloid, no representation is made regarding the accuracy of this presentation.

1951
Deluxe

70 A Tudor	52,865	78,030
72 C Business Coupe	9,753	8,577
73 A Fordor	17,600	30,917
Total Deluxe	*80,218*	*117,524*

Custom

60 Victoria	—	110,282
70 B Tudor	45,999	228,797
72 B Club Coupe	5,977	40,056
70 C Crestliner	—	6,858
73 B Fordor	14,814	186,544
76 Convertible Coupe	—	37,034
79 B Station Wagon	625	26,042
Total Custom	*67,415*	*635,613*
Total Passenger Cars		*900,770*

1952
Mainline

70 A Tudor	36,200	55,960
72 C Business Coupe	6,270	5,316
73 A Fordor	18.033	29,434
59 A Ranch Wagon	9,791	28,223
Total Mainline	*70,294*	*118,933*

Customline & Crestline

60 B Victoria	—	87,964
70 B Tudor	44,212	156,013
72 B Club Coupe	5,663	24,156
73 B Fordor	35,528	189,177
76 B Sunliner	—	25,054
79 C Country Squire	—	6,360
79 D Country Sedan	46	14,126
Total Customline & Crestline	*85,454*	*502,850*
Total Passenger Cars		*777,531*

1953
Mainline

70 A Tudor	82,699	61,494
72 C Business Coupe	9,618	5,542
73 A Fordor	32,570	32,338
59 A Ranch Wagon	17,425	45,041
Total Mainline	*142,312*	*144,415*

Customlines

70 B Tudor	82,269	207,113
72 B Club Coupe	9,775	31,912
73 B Fordor	71,130	270,693
59 B Ranch Wagon	490	928
79 B Country Sedan	165	36,790
Total Customlines	*163,829*	*547,436*

Crestline

60 B Victoria	534	122,069
60 F Skyliner	81	1,047
73 C Fordor	2,390	9,736
76 B Sunliner	1	39,944
79 C Country Squire	4	10,387
Total Crestline	*3,010*	*183,183*
Total Passenger Cars		*1,184,185*

1954

Mainline	SIX	V-8
70 A Tudor	79,541	60,280
70 D Business Tudor	8,416	4,318
73 A Fordor	34,185	28,761
Total Mainline	*122,142*	*93,359*

Customline	SIX	V-8
70 B Tudor	95,807	269,660
73 B Fordor	64,196	239,867
Total Customline	*160,003*	*509,527*

Fairlane	SIX	V-8
60 B Victoria	4,693	109,126
64 A Crown Victoria	4	5,424
64 B Crown, Victoria Glass Top	330	11,929
70 C Club Sedan	160	27,448
73 C Town Sedan	9,017	122,384
76 B Sunliner	1,000	40,071
Total Fairlane	*15,205*	*316,382*

	SIX	V-8
40 A Thunderbird		*3,546*

Station Wagons	SIX	V-8
59 A ML Ranch Wagon	20,694	32,071
59 B CL Ranch Wagon	8,643	34,642
79 B 8-pass. Country Sedan	5,275	52,667
79 D 6-pass. Country Sedan	392	5,119
79 C Country Squire	352	14,743
Total Station Wagons	*35,356*	*139,242*
Total Passenger Cars		*1,394,762*

1955

Mainline	SIX	272 V-8	292 V-8	312 V-8
70 A Tudor	44,644	31,560		556
70 D Business Tudor	6,578	2,246		8
73 A Fordor	25,242	19,502		399
Total Mainline	*76,464*	*53,308*		*963*

Customline	SIX	272 V-8	292 V-8	312 V-8
70 B Tudor	57,239	204,927		352
73 B Fordor	45,378	227,616		188
Total Customline	*102,617*	*432,543*		*540*

Fairlane	SIX	272 V-8	292 V-8	312 V-8
57 A Victoria Fordor	18		1,739	2
64 A Crown Victoria	114		32,361	4
64 B Crown Victoria Glass Top	59		2,260	1
64 C Victoria	638		160,746	16
70 C Club Sedan	1,963		214,587	41
73 C Town Sedan	4,856		312,191	42
76 B Sunliner	264		64,286	
Total Fairlane	*7,912*		*788,170*	*106*

	SIX	272 V-8	292 V-8	312 V-8
Thunderbird			*12,810*	*2,850*

Station Wagons	SIX	272 V-8	292 V-8	312 V-8
59 A Ranch Wagon	15,397		29,715	2
59 D Custom Ranch Wagon	6,438		46,371	2
59 C Parklane	80		11,682	
79 B 8-pass. Country Sedan	3,643		65,714	11
79 D 6-pass. Country Sedan	5,055		74,911	4
79 C Country Squire	126		27,088	2
Total Station Wagons	*30,739*		*255,481*	*21*
Total By Engine	*217,732*	*485,851*	*1,056,605*	*4,336*
Total Passenger Cars				*1,764,524*

1956

Custom	SIX	272 V-8	292 V-8	312 V-8
70 A Tudor	55,168	51,842	2,576	2,927
70 D Business Tudor	5,770	1,487	68	60
73 A Fordor	25,626	24,667	1,318	1,600
Total Custom	*86,564*	*77,996*	*3,959*	*4,587*

Custom 300	SIX	272 V-8	292 V-8	312 V-8
70 B Tudor	27,211	129,378	14,006	4,979
73 B Fordor	21,573	116,658	6,173	7,180
Total Custom 300	*48,784*	*246,036*	*20,179*	*12,159*

Fairlane	SIX	272 V-8	292 V-8	312 V-8
57 B Town Victoria	90		3,978	2,566
58 A Town Sedan	800		17,999	5,995
63 B Club Victoria	339		19,584	7,057
64 A Tudor Club Sedan	575		16,481	3,624
Total Fairlane	*1,804*		*58,042*	*18,842*

Fairlane 500	SIX	272 V-8	292 V-8	312 V-8
57 A Town Victoria	324		25,252	19,767
58 B Town Sedan	2,785		122,776	36,666
63 A Club Victoria	839		106,735	47,334
64 B Tudor Club Sedan	1,298		82,982	18,651
76 B Sunliner	256		34,356	18,361
Total Fairlane 500	*5,502*		*372,101*	*140,779*

	SIX	272 V-8	292 V-8	312 V-8
Thunderbird			*1,158*	*17,359*

Station Wagons	SIX	272 V-8	292 V-8	312 V-8
59 A Ranch Wagon	16,341		32,297	1,725
59 B Del Rio	3,826		35,863	6,034
79 C 8-pass. Country Sedan	2,195		37,104	12,685
79 D 6-pass. Country Sedan	4,814		65,590	18,234
79 E Country Squire	81		14,464	6,438
Total Station Wagons	*27,257*		*185,318*	*45,116*
Total By Engine	*169,911*	*324,032*	*640,757*	*238,842*
Total Passenger Cars				*1,373,542*

PRODUCTION FIGURES

1957

	SIX	292 V-8	312 V-8
Custom			
70 A Tudor	69,012	31,045	4,205
70 D Business Tudor	4,574	1,341	112
73 A Fordor	34,508	24,667	2,952
Total Custom	108,044	57,053	7,269
Custom 300			
70 B Tudor	34,880	96,308	5,752
73 B Fordor	34,519	124,722	6,939
Total Custom 300	69,401	221,030	12,692
Fairlane			
57 B Town Victoria	295	1,178	5,868
58 A Town Sedan	3,002	7,896	29,018
63 B Club Victoria	1,245	3,209	16,446
64 A Tudor Club Sedan	3,156	5,473	18,293
Total Fairlane	7,698	17,756	69,625
Fairlane 500			
51 A Skyliner		9,161	18,442
57 A Town Victoria	994	40,115	32,542
58 B Town Sedan	4,374	128,482	64,884
63 A Club Victoria	2,615	99,522	70,797
64 B Club Sedan	2,275	58,272	19,602
76 B Sunliner	783	38,957	36,047
Total Fairlane 500	11,043	374,509	247,264
Station Wagons			
59 A Ranch Wagon	24,025	29,224	1,739
59 B Del Rio	4,122	26,218	4,659
59 C 9-pass. Country Sedan	3,596	24,013	11,154
79 A Fordor Ranch Wagon	2,720	5,511	489
79 D 6-pass. Country Sedan	8,428	90,221	28,593
79 E Country Squire	267	14,644	9,856
Total Station Wagons	43,158	189,831	56,490
Thunderbird			
40 A 1957 Model		1,288	14,155
Total By Engine	239,344		
Total Passenger Cars			

1958

	SIX	332 V-8	352 V-8	361 V-8
Custom 300				
58 E Fordor	82,726	84,371	6,444	7,793
64 F Tudor	113,786	66,553	3,555	4,292
64 G Business Tudor	3,573	831	15	
Total Custom 300	200,085	152,115	10,014	12,085
Fairlane				
58 A Town Fordor	9,893	44,997	1,997	1,503
64 A Club Tudor	11,006	31,735	3,386	1,205
Total Fairlane	20,899	76,732		2,708
Fairlane 500				
57 A Fordor Victoria	765	2,568	14,701	6,122
58 B Fordor Sedan	3,793	8,342	57,818	13,115
63 A Tudor Victoria	1,766	5,297	39,201	15,705
64 B Tudor Sedan	1,374	3,521	16,463	2,539
Total Fairlane 500	7,698	19,728	128,183	37,481
Station Wagons				
59 A Ranch Wagon				
59 C Del Rio				
71 E 9-pass. Country Sedan				
71 F 6-pass. Country Sedan				
71 G Country Squire				
71 H Ranch Wagon				
Total Station Wagons				5,405
Thunderbird				
Total By Engine	327,712			
Total Passenger Cars	1,066,322			

1958 (cont.)

	SIX	292 V-8	352 V-8	430 V-8
Galaxie				
51 A Skyliner Galaxie				367
54 A Fordor Galaxie	557	7,045	5,008	6,124
64 H Tudor Galaxie	7,747	13,770	2,808	4,432
65 A Tudor Galaxie	2,971	2,894		699
Total Galaxie	61,102	22,885	9,495	28,566
Station Wagons				
59 C Ranch Wagon	21,681	7,927	5,773	9,954
59 D Country Sedan	1,632	2,533	2,596	4,554
71 E 9-pass. Country Sedan	2,816	3,737	2,921	2,517
71 F 4-Door Country Sedan	5,730	12,843		6,960
71 G Country Squire	290	1,750		3,736
71 H Ranch Wagon	17,400	10,408	10,822	502
Total Station Wagons	49,549	37,198	11,706	94,690
Thunderbird				
Thunderbird (430 V-8)				50
Total By Engine	279,898	306,331	141,944	
Total Passenger Cars				1,038,560

1959

	SIX	292 V-8	352 V-8	430 V-8
Fairlane & Custom 300	6	9	15	
54 A Fordor Custom 300	98,390	155,667	41,104	6,030
58 F Fordor Custom 300	10	45,720	7,147	2,530
58 E Fordor Fairlane	105,666	92,689	17,784	8,919
64 F Tudor Fairlane	2,759	587	23	
Total Fairlane & Custom 300	206,831	364,708	126,108	
Fairlane 500				
58 A Fordor Sedan	20,639	79,175	6,030	
64 A Tudor Sedan	18,249	34,529	2,530	
Total Fairlane 500	38,888	113,704	8,560	2,703
Galaxie				
54 A Fordor Sedan	9,914	119,247	41,104	3,968
62 A Tudor Sedan	6,794		7,147	
75 A Fordor Victoria	1,553	37,995	16,159	6,032
63 A Tudor Victoria	5,003	92,689	41,261	14,734
76 B Sunliner	1,485	28,275	17,784	7,523
51 A Skyliner		4,362	2,703	1,419
Total Galaxie	24,749	364,708	126,108	30,864
Station Wagons				
59 C Ranch Wagon	21,350	23,608	856	
59 D Country Sedan	8,225	18,900	6,032	
71 E 9-pass. Country Squire	6,676	68,374	14,734	
71 F 6-pass. Country Squire	533	16,186	7,523	
71 G Country Squire	25,460	38,510	1,419	
71 H Fordor Ranch Wagon				
Total Station Wagons	57,244	165,578	30,864	
Thunderbird			52,135	70,278
Total Passenger Cars			5,445	1,427,835